Rosie's Walk

by Pat Hutchins
Macmillan, [1968] 1971

Summary: Rosie went for a walk, unaware of the fox trailing behind her.

Language Arts:

Synonyms: What words mean the same as *walk*?

Antonyms: What words mean the opposite of *predator*?

Categorization: Map words that have something in common with the category *prey*.

> meat eat attack
> trick —— **prey** —— predator
> food nature

Homonyms: What are other spellings/meanings for the words *yard and past*?

Context: Using the context of the story, what words make sense in the blanks?

Rosie the _____ went for a _____ across the _____ .

Dictionary usage: Find the words *hen* and *fox* in the dictionary. What are their definitions?

Parts of speech: Which words name something?

| hen | yard | over | mill | fence |
| across | pond | past | under | haystack |

Structural analysis: Which words have the same /o/ sound as in *Rosie*?

| through | got | pond | over |

Chickens
and
Eggs

Illustrated by Lyn Hope

Watten/Poe
Teaching Resource Center

Published by
Teaching Resource Center
P.O. Box 1509
San Leandro, CA 94577

Printed in the United States of America
ISBN: 1–56785–013–8

Contents

The Basic Teaching Strategies

In the development of this theme you will find such phrases as **brainstorm for, develop in the pocket chart, sort and classify**, etc. To help clarify these phrases we have listed these basic teaching strategies and have given a brief description of each.

Fill with language:

This is when we read to the children. We read not only stories but poetry and factual information as well. We begin with a discussion of the illustrations to develop as much oral language as possible. We stop periodically to provide the opportunity for the child to anticipate and predict what might happen next. We also read a selection many times over to help make that selection become a part of the child. We feel strongly that we must continually *fill the child with language* as we move ahead with the theme.

Chanting:

Children need to work orally with the patterns of language. The primary way to do this with very young children is by chanting. This technique helps instill the rhythm and structure of language which then becomes a part of their everyday speech.

One way to chant is by using the my turn, your turn technique. The teacher reads a phrase and the children echo this phrase. The teacher tracks (runs hand under the text, pointing to each word) as the chanting takes place. Children may chant using the whole text (pictures, pictures and words, or words alone), or merely chant a repetitive phrase ("Not I," said the dog.) Chanting may be done using big books, charts, brainstorming ideas, pocket chart activities, trade books, etc. Songs and poems should also be included. When working with songs and poetry, we often add rhythmic hand movements which help instill the rhythm of the language and enhances the memorization.

Brainstorming:

Brainstorming is when children orally respond to a question posed by the teacher with the results usually being recorded where they may be seen by the children. This gives the teacher an insight into the children's knowledge. We usually begin a theme by brainstorming for what the children know about a given subject. A lack of ideas indicates that the children may need a *refill* of language and knowledge. The brainstorming is continuously being added to as the theme is developed.

Brainstorming is a whole class activity. The teacher begins by asking a question such as "What is green?" and elicits responses from the children. As the children respond, the teacher draws the appropriate pictures on the chalkboard and the children chant. **Note:** at the beginning of the kindergarten year, draw a picture only. No words are needed.

After the brainstorming, again chant all the pictures that were drawn: "A leaf is green. A turtle is green. Grass is green. A car is green." As the year progresses you will want to add words to the brainstorming:

Most brainstorming needs to be saved! As you work through a theme you will be continually referring to these ideas. Copy the brainstorming onto cards or chart paper. The cards may be displayed using masking tape, sticky side out. The chart may be used for matching and rebuilding. At a later date the chart may be cut apart and made into a strip book.

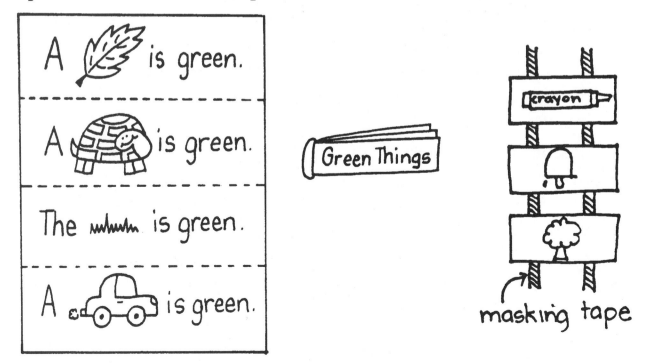

Another example of a brainstorming technique is to record ideas in categories that are not labeled. After the pattern is obvious, the children tell where to record the next idea. This method helps stimulate the children's thinking.

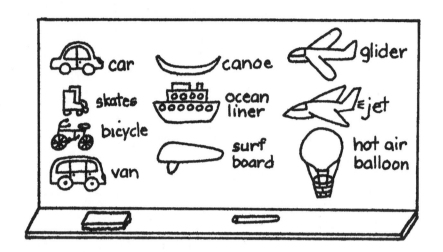

Sorting and Classifying:

 This when children look for likenesses and differences and put things together that are alike in some manner. The ideas from brainstorming activities are ideal for sorting and classifying. We usually begin classifying with groups of four to six children, with each group having about twenty cards or items to sort.

After this small group sorting activity, the whole class regroups and chants. Example: we classified according to color and then chanted, "A chair is green. An olive is green. A fat frog is green, etc." Gradually, we work toward activities that will involve individual classifications. The results of these activities may be graphed, producing either a real graph or a pictorial graph.[1]

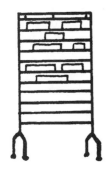

Develop in the Pocket Chart:

We use a pocket chart made of clear acetate and nylon.[2] You may use sentence strips or tagboard cards (laminated or contacted for a longer life) with the pocket chart. Whole texts, repeated phrases or pictures only may be used. There are a variety of ways to use the pocket chart. We listed our favorites:

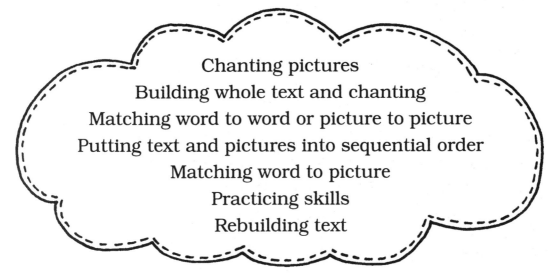

Chanting pictures
Building whole text and chanting
Matching word to word or picture to picture
Putting text and pictures into sequential order
Matching word to picture
Practicing skills
Rebuilding text

When we are developing a lesson in the pocket chart, we usually insert the appropriate pictures, or text and pictures, and then have the children chant **many** times. We may ask the children to hide their eyes and then we take something out of the text or merely turn it over.

The children then decide what is missing and chant to see if they are correct. We then take more than one word, picture, or phrase out (or turn them over) and repeat the process. The final task is to rebuild the entire text.

Samples:

Step 1:   Chanting pictures
           "A leaf is green."

Step 2:	Build whole text and chant: "A leaf is green."	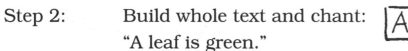
Step 3:	Matching word to word or picture to picture: (Children match above, below, or on top of)	
Step 4:	Putting text and pictures into sequential order:	
Step 5:	Matching word to picture:	
Step 6:	Practicing skills:	

- Find the word that says *green.*
- Find the word that says *is.*
- Find the word that comes before *green.*
- Find the word that comes after *is.*
- What sound do you hear at the beginning of the word *leaf?*

Step 7: Rebuilding: all pictures and text are distributed to the children and the complete story is built again in the pocket chart. Children read the text from the pocket chart, checking for accuracy.

Tracking:

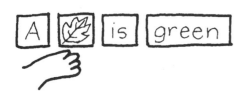

This involves moving your hand under and pointing to each word as it is read. This helps develop left to right progression as well as one-to-one correspondence between the printed text and the spoken word.

Big Books:

These are enlarged versions of books, poems or songs. The print must be large enough so that it may be seen by the entire class. The enlarged print allows us to track as we read and helps to develop one-to-one correspondence. Many of the activities used with the pocket chart may also be used with big books. We laminate the pages of teacher-prepared big books and bind them with loose leaf rings. The rings may be taken out and the pages shuffled so that the children may sequence the big book. For obvious reasons **do not** number the pages. These books are really loved and used over and over by the children.

Extensions:

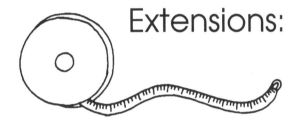

These are activities we practice what we learned during brain-storming, reading, chanting, and the various pocket chart activities. We try to incorporate the following:

Individual booklets – Each child makes his/her own booklet and should have the opportunity to read and track before taking it home.

Class book – Each child contributes a page and the book is kept in the classroom library.

Drama – Children act out the activity with **all** children taking **all** the parts. (a bit noisy but very effective)

Art – Children make illustrations for bulletin boards, booklets, plays, etc., using as many different kinds of art media as possible.

Make-a-play – Children retell a story by manipulating characters they have made.

Writing – All writing activities need to be extensively developed orally **first.**

1. Using a structure or frame, the children fill in the blanks by taking the ideas from the brainstorming activities.

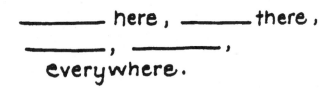

2. Creating innovations: children orally rewrite a familiar text using their own words. Example: (change "Brown bear, brown bear, what do you see?" to "Octopus, Octopus, what do you see?") This can be an individual or a whole group activity. The teacher may need to take dictation for the very young child.

3. Dictation: children individually illustrate and the teacher transcribes for them.

Draw with me – This is a whole class activity where language development is the goal. We do not consider this an art lesson. All the children are working with individual chalkboards at this time. We ask the children to name all the parts that need to be included to draw a specific object. A sample follows on the next page.

"What do we need to make a house?"

"A door"

"A roof"

"Windows"

(continue until entire picture is completed)

Individual sequencing – This is when each child puts pictures or a text into a specific order. This is usually a *cut and paste* activity. It varies in difficulty. We begin with pictures only, then pictures with the text, and finally the text alone. We also put the text in sequence with numerals, words, and pictures.

Pictures only:

Pictures with text:

Numeral, text and picture:

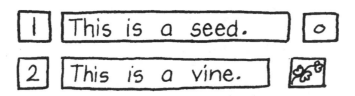

Homework – This is when we try to involve the family. The homework is occasional and we include a detailed explanation. This activity is returned to class and used for chanting, classifying booklet making or other language activities.

An example might be:

Dear Parents,

Our language arts theme this month is centered around plants. This week we are learning about seeds. Your child needs to bring a picture of something that grows from a seed. You may help your child draw or find a picture in a magazine. Please return the picture tomorrow.

Thank you for helping!

A follow-up activity might include sorting and classifying these pictures according to whether the plant produces food or not, i.e., flower, grapes, oak tree, oranges, etc. A booklet can then be made including all the homework pictures or individual booklets may be made from each classification.

————————————————————————————————————

1. Baratta-Lorton, Mary. *Mathematics Their Way*, Addison-Wesley Publishing Company, Reading, MA 1976.
2. Available from **Teaching Resource Center**, P.O. Box 1509, 14023 Catalina St., San Leandro, CA 94577.

Theme At A Glance

Trade Books & Big Books

Across The Stream
Chickens Aren't The Only Ones
Flap Your Wings
Hattie And The Fox
Me Too
Not Now Said The Cow
Rosie's Walk
Seven Eggs
The Chick And The Duckling
The Chicken Book
The Golden Egg Book
The Little Red Hen
Too Many Eggs
Where's My Easter Egg?

Where's The Egg?

Class Books & Booklets

Hattie And The Fox Rewrite
Strip Book - "Chickens..."
Strip Book - "Peck, Peck, Peck!"
Talking Chicks (Thumprint Book)
What Is Oviparous?

A Chick...(Factual Booklet)
Eggs In A Nest
Me Too
Rosie's Walk
Seven Eggs
The Chicken Book (Pop-up)
The Little Red Hen
Where's The Egg?

Songs

Little Red Hen Song

Art

Oviparous Bulletin Board
Thumbprint Art - Talking Chicks Class Book
"Who Will Help Me?" Directed Drawing

 # Science & Math

Accordian Book- Bread Making   Facts About Chickens & Eggs
Accordian Book- Egg Hatching Sequence   Ordinal Numbers- Seven Eggs
AIMS Activities   Sort & Classify- Oviparous Animals
Bake A Cake   Yeast Experiment
Come With Me Science -"Domesticated Birds"

 # Drama

Humpty Dumpty
Little Red Hen Finger Puppets
Little Red Hen Stick Puppets
Not Now Said The Cow
Rosie's Walk
The Chick And The Duckling

LYN

Introduction

This theme is written in a specific sequence, but it is merely a suggestion. You need not follow this exact order. Choose those activities that best suit your classroom. Please note that the last activity is about Easter. We like to use this theme at Easter time but it is not necessary. If you use it at a different time, omit the final activity.

Our lessons describe several ways to develop a story but this does not limit the number of times we repeat the activity. We don't teach a song and sing it only once – nor do we work with a book only one time. After several repetitions we like to put the pocket chart pictures, words and book in a large envelope that has a reduced copy of the words and pictures on the front. We place them in a basket where the children are able to rebuild these activities on their own and read the book independently.

As we are developing our themes, we gather materials wherever we can find them. Obtaining the materials is quite easy (and fun); the difficulty lies in narrowing the selections so that we include a variety of teaching strategies. We select a book for its strength and for the manner in which it can enrich the theme.

At the time this book went to press, all the books we have developed were in print. However, books are going in and out of print all the time. If you cannot locate a particular book, try the public library, your school library or contact a local bookstore and they might be able to track the selection down for you.

Materials:

- *The Little Red Hen* by Paul Galdone
- As many other versions of *The Little Red Hen* as you can locate
- Blacklines 1–2 for the pocket chart
- Blacklines 3–7 for individual booklets
- Four pieces of 5" x 5" tagboard to mount blackline 1
- Twelve pieces of 4" x 5" tagboard to mount blacklines 2–3
- Red construction paper for the booklet covers, two per child
- Sentence strips
- Contact paper or laminating film
- Colored felt pens
- Materials for yeast experiment (recipe under Procedure)
- Blacklines 8–11 for stick puppets
- Four pieces of 8½" x 11" tagboard for mounting puppets
- *The Little Red Hen* pocket chart activity available from
     McCracken Educational Services, 17379 21A Avenue,
     Surrey, B.C. V4B 5E7 (optional)
- Blackline 12 for finger puppets
- 3" x 2" construction paper, four per child, for the finger puppets
- Blacklines 13–16 for a directed drawing booklet
- Individual chalkboards, chalk and erasers
- *"Not Now!" Said the Cow* by Joanne Oppenheim
- *Ed Emberley's Drawing book of Animals* by Ed Emberley

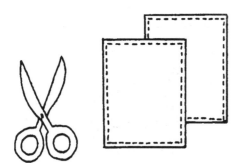

Preparation:

1. Color, cut and mount the pictures from blacklines 1–2. Contact or laminate.

2. Make four separate sentence strips that say:

   Little Red Hen _____ the wheat.

3. Make two separate sentence strips that say:

   Little Red Hen _____ the treat.

4. On separate word cards, print the following:

   plants   tends   cuts

   grinds   bakes   eats

5. Duplicate blackline 3, one per child, for the Little Red Hen booklet pictures. **Duplicate one more copy** to use in the pocket chart. Color this one, cut and mount on tagboard. Contact or laminate.

6. Duplicate blackline 4, two per child, to make the first four pages of *The Little Red Hen* booklet. Cut in half.

7. Duplicate blackline 5, one per child, to make the last two pages of *The Little Red Hen* booklet. Cut these in half also.
   Note: these last two pages refer to the *wheat* as *treat*.

8. For a class of thirty-two, make eight copies of blackline 6. Cut into fourths so that each child has one set of words to use for *The Little Red Hen* booklet.

2

9. Duplicate blackline 7, one per child, on red construction paper for *The Little Red Hen* booklet cover.

10. Staple each booklet cover to a blank piece of red construction paper so that when the children cut the covers they will both be the same size.

11. Color, cut, mount and laminate blacklines 8–11 to make the stick puppets. After they are laminated, staple each puppet to a tongue depressor.

12. On white construction paper, duplicate blackline 12 for the finger puppets. For a class of thirty-two make sixteen duplicates and cut in half.

13. Duplicate blacklines 13–16, one per child, for the "directed drawing" booklet. Add a construction paper cover and staple in the order of the blacklines.

14. On sentence strips print the following and cut into individual word cards. Be sure the question mark is on a word card by itself as you will be placing housework pictures between the word *me* and the question mark.

> **"Who will help me?" said the Little Red Hen.**
> **"Not I," said the dog.**
> **"Not I," said the cat.**
> **"Not I," said the mouse.**
> **"Then I will," said the Little Red Hen.**
>   **And she did.**

15. On sentence strips print the numerals 1–6 and cut into individual cards.

16. Print the names of the children in your class on individual word cards.

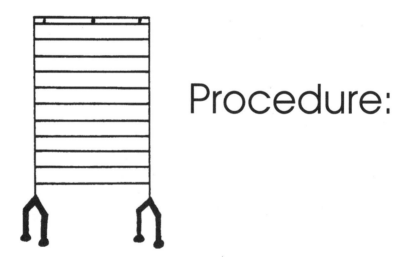

Procedure:

Part 1

1. Read and enjoy *The Little Red Hen* by Paul Galdone.
2. Divide your class into three sections: a dog section, a cat section and a mouse section. Read the book again. The teacher reads the part of the Little Red Hen while each group joins in with the repeated *"Not I"* sentence at the appropriate time.

3. Place the numeral cards 1–6 in the pocket chart. Place the pictures from blackline 2 where they can be easily seen and obtained by the children.

4. The children sequence the story in the pocket chart by placing the appropriate picture next to the numeral card.

5. Remove the numeral cards and distribute them to six children.

6. Ask the children to cover their eyes while you rearrange the pictures in the pocket chart.

7. The children then match the appropriate numeral with the pictures in the pocket chart. **Note:** this is harder than it sounds. You may have to lend a hand if the going gets rough.

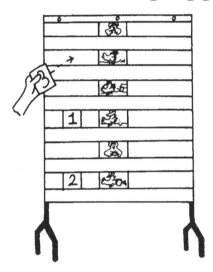

8. Reread *The Little Red Hen.* The children join in on all the repeated phrases.

9. Develop these repeated phrases and the corresponding pictures (blackline 1) in the pocket chart.

* leave 1st pocket empty for the question								
"Not	I,"	said	the	dog.	🐕			
"Not	I,"	said	the	cat.	🐈			
"Not	I,"	said	the	mouse.	🐁			
"Then	I	will,"	said	the	little	Red	Hen.	🐔
	And	she	did.					

10. Brainstorm on the chalkboard for all the work the Little Red Hen did (from the Galdone version). Now ask the children to think of other housework for which the Little Red Hen might need help. At this point *you have two choices. You may use the housework pictures from the McCracken Pocket Chart Activity or you may draw your own.* Be sure to add the children's brainstorming to this set of cards.

11. For first grade, print the brainstormed housework phrases so they match the pictures you have drawn. If you are using the McCracken packet, the words are included.

12. In the top of the pocket chart, place the words, *"Who will help me?" said the Little Red Hen.*

13. Display the housework pictures so they may be easily obtained by the children. The children take turns choosing pictures and placing them in the pocket chart. Each time the whole class reads, using a housework picture to complete the question. The children then answer each question by reading the *"Not I"* phrases. For first grade, add the words next to the picture or replace the picture with the words.

14. Your children will enjoy having their names substituted for the Dog, Cat and Mouse. Here is a perfect place to brainstorm for things their mothers and fathers ask them to do around the house. After you have completed this brainstorming, print the chores on sentence strips and re-teach the lesson in the pocket chart using the children's names and their chores.

Note: Because of the length of *The Little Red Hen*, we have chosen to add extensions throughout Activity 1.

Extension 1: Directed drawing booklet. This booklet takes us about four days as we develop one character each day. The repeated phrases that are illustrated under Procedure, step 9, should be in the pocket chart as the children work on this booklet.

A. Distribute the prepared directed drawing booklets (made from blacklines 13–16) to the children. Working with the whole class, read the first page of the booklet. Determine which words are missing by referring back to the pocket chart. Using the words in the pocket chart as a guide, the children print the missing words in the appropriate blanks. Set these booklets aside for step B and C.

B. This step is going to be a language lesson rather than an art lesson. We ask the children to name all the attributes that need to be included to draw the particular animal on which you are working. As each attribute is mentioned, the teacher illustrates that particular part of the animal on the chalkboard, adding one attribute at a time until the animal is completed.

What does a dog have?

"A tail"

"Ears"

"A head"

You may wish to chant all the brainstormed attributes when you are finished: "A dog has a tail. A dog has ears. A dog has a head." etc.

Note: For drawing ideas, you might wish to use *Ed Emberley's Drawing Book Of Animals* for the pictures of the hen, cat, dog and mouse. Whatever source you choose, be sure to make the animal look the same as the one you will have the children draw in their booklets.

C. Distribute individual chalkboards, chalk and erasers to the class. Going step by step, direct the children in the drawing of the animal (dog). The teacher uses a chalkboard to demonstrate while the children use their individual boards. The class needs this practice time before they draw the animal in their booklet.

D. Each child illustrates the dog on the first page in their directed drawing booklets. This can be done step-by-step if you wish.

E. Continue developing each animal in the same way.

F. A title for the cover might be *Who Will Help Me?* The children can use the hen or all four characters for the cover illustration.

G. Read the completed booklets together and take home.

Procedure – Part 2

1. Review by rereading the story *The Little Red Hen.* Choose four children to help retell the story by chanting their parts.
2. Distribute the stick puppets to four children. The teacher is the narrator during this first dramatization, which serves as a model for the class. Now choose a child to be the narrator and have each of the four children choose friends to take their places. The new cast dramatizes the story, using the stick puppets. Continue in this manner until all the children have had a turn.

Extension 2: Finger puppets

A. Distribute one set of puppets (made from blackline 12) and the 3" x 2" pieces of construction paper to the children. (Each child needs four pieces of construction paper.)
B. The children color the four characters and cut them out.
C. Using the small pieces of construction paper, direct the children in making four tubes that will fit their fingers and then glue the puppet character to the tubes.

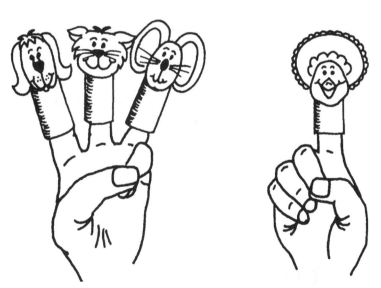

D. Using these finger puppets, have the children find a partner and dramatize the story to each other.
E. Encourage the children to take the puppets home and dramatize the story for their family.

Procedure – Part 3

1. Ask the children what the Little Red Hen did with the wheat to prepare it for the treat. As the children name each step, place that picture in the pocket chart. (These pictures are from blackline 3.)

2. Place the word cards (plants, tends, cuts, grinds, bakes, eats) at the bottom of the pocket chart. Using phonetic clues, help the children match the words to the appropriate pictures.

3. Distribute the six word cards and six pictures to the class. Have the children find their partner and replace the cards and pictures in the pocket chart in the correct order. If you do this activity a few more times, each child will have a turn.

4. Remove the pictures and word cards and place them at the bottom of the pocket chart. At the top of the pocket chart place the four **"Little Red Hen _____ the wheat."** sentences and the two **"Little Red Hen _____ the treat."** sentences in the pocket chart.

Little Red Hen _____ the wheat.

Little Red Hen _____ the wheat.

Little Red Hen _____ the wheat.

Little Red Hen _____ the wheat.

Little Red Hen _____ the treat.

Little Red Hen _____ the treat.

eats   grinds   plants

tends   cuts   bakes

5. The children now place the appropriate words and pictures in the pocket chart and read. Leave this in the pocket chart for Extension 3.

6. Brainstorm for other treats that could be made with wheat. List these on the chalkboard and chant, "_____ is made with wheat."

Extension 3: Individual Booklets

A. The children cut out the booklet covers. (blackline 7)

B. Using the pocket chart as a guide, the children glue the missing words on the booklet pages (blacklines 4–6). Caution the children to be careful as two pages refer to *treat* while the other four pages refer to *wheat.*

C. Direct the children to color the pictures (blackline 3), cut apart and glue to the appropriate pages.

D. The children sequence the pages, add the covers and staple as shown.

E. Read the booklet together. Choose a friend and read the booklet again. Take the booklet home and read to the family.

Procedure – Part 4

1. Read as many other versions of *The Little Red Hen* as you are able to locate. Compare and contrast the characters, the language and the treat.

2. If you did not make the *Little Red Hen* booklet, a "mapping" activity is fun to do at this point. Cut a 4″ x 18″ strip of white

11

construction paper and fold it in six equal sections, accordion style. Brainstorm for all the things the Little Red Hen did to the wheat and then the children illustrate each job on a different section of the paper. When the children are finished, they can retell the story using this *map* as a guide.

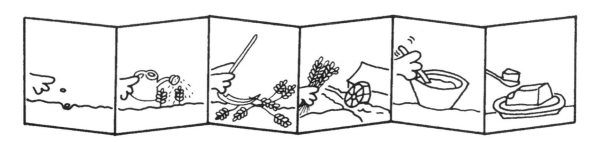

Extension 4: Yeast Experiment

A. Ask the children to tell you everything they know about yeast.

B. Have a discussion about bakers adding yeast to the flour to make the product light and airy. If you did not use yeast, the product would still be tasty but it would be solid and heavy.
(If you can locate a baker, invite the baker to your classroom to share first-hand knowledge.)

C. Do the following experiment.
Dissolve 1 ounce of yeast and 1 teaspoon of sugar in 1¼ cups of warm water. Mix this with 2 cups of flour. Let the dough stand in a warm place and watch how the dough rises.

D. Discuss the chemical reaction that has taken place and relate that to the products that are made with yeast. The yeast has changed the sugar into alcohol and carbon dioxide. Bubbles of the gas are trapped in the dough. During baking the alcohol evaporates but the gas bubbles stay in the bread. Examine a piece of bread, looking at the holes. Have the children tell in their own words what made these holes.

E. If your schedule permits, you may wish to bake bread, pretzels, or rolls. If you do not have the facilities or the time, it is fun to bring in different kinds of bread and have a *Little Red Hen* tasting party.

Extension 5: Music

A. Teach *Red Hen's Song,* found in the kindergarten teacher's manual of the 1989 Silver Burdett Music Series.

B. Substitute the words and the characters to match the version we have used.

C. When the children have learned the song, have them take turns singing the various parts, with the entire class singing, "And she did, and she did, and she did."

Extension 6: *"Not Now!" Said the Cow*

A. Ask the following: if the Little Red Hen found a corn seed instead of wheat, what would have grown and what might she have made? (cornbread, corn muffins, cornmeal mush, corn on the cob, hominy, etc.)

B. Read and enjoy the book, *"Not Now!" Said the Cow.*

C. Review the steps the Little Red Hen went through before she was able to bake the bread. List these steps on the chalkboard. Now list the steps the crow used before he could pop the corn. Compare and contrast these. Which were the same? Which were different? Why?

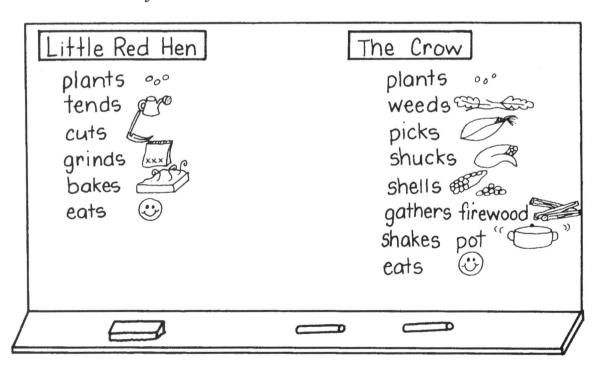

D. Talk about rhyme and read the story again, asking the children to clap when they hear a rhyming pair of words. Stop and ask a child to tell the class the two rhyming words. You may wish to list these on the chalkboard, put them on word cards for the pocket chart or merely discuss them orally.

E. This story is a must for drama. On sentence strips, print the repeated sentence of each animal and also what these animals said when the corn was popped. We suggest that you print each animal's text in a different color as this will help the students find their parts. (This may be too difficult for beginning kindergarten.)

F. Divide the class into eight groups. Each group will take the part of one of the animals. (cow, sheep, chicks, donkey, bunny, hog, cat and mare.) The teacher will be the crow (hee hee) and the narrator.

G. Using the pocket chart as a guide, read the story again with the children acting out the various parts.

H. If you really want to get into this story, you may wish to have the children make masks for the characters and put on the "play" for another class.

I. Make popcorn! You may wish to bring in several ears of corn – some dried and some fresh. *If you are going to pop this dried corn, be sure that it is from the type of corn plant that is raised for popcorn.*

Activity 2 *Rosie's Walk*

Materials:

- *Rosie's Walk* by Pat Hutchins
- 12" x 18" red construction paper for booklet cover, one per child
- 9" x 12" light blue construction paper for booklet pages, seven per child
- 9" x 3" black construction paper for Rosie's home in barn, one per child
- 10½" x 1" black construction paper for barn front, two per child
- Raffia or straw for the hay
- Brads for the mill
- Blackline 17 for the silos, two silos per child
- Blackline 18 for the barn top and the haystack, one per child
- Blackline 19 for the mill, one per child
- Blackline 20 for the beehive, one per child
- Googly eyes for Rosie, one per child
- Feathers for Rosie
- Blacklines 21–22 for the pocket chart and for Rosie's feet and beak
- Seven pieces of 4" x 5" tagboard cards
- Sentence strips
- Felt pens
- Contact paper or laminating film
- Wallpaper scraps in shades of brown, orange, yellow or tan
- Corn kernels
- 9" x 6" blue construction paper to make the pond, one per child

15

- 9" x ½" brown construction paper strips for the fence, two per child
- 3" x ¾" brown construction paper strips for the fence posts, three per child
- String, one 7" piece per child
- Railroad board or cardboard for Rosie's body
- Light brown construction paper to make the fox heads

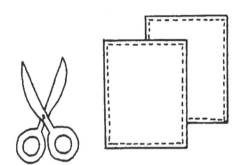

Preparation:

1. Duplicate blackline 17 on red construction paper, one per child. (Each child will need two silos for the booklet.)
2. Duplicate blacklines 18–19 on yellow construction paper, one per child.
3. Duplicate blackline 20 on white construction paper, one per child. **Note:** blacklines 21–22 are for the pocket chart. Blackline 22 also has the feet and beak for Rosie. **Please be sure to make a copy of blackline 22 before you color the last pocket chart picture!**

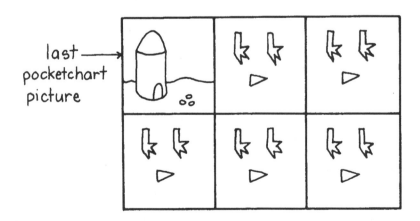

last pocketchart picture

4. Color, cut and mount the pocket chart pictures from blacklines 21 and 22. Contact or laminate.

5. Using the copy you made from blackline 22, duplicate the feet and beaks for your class on orange construction paper, one set per child.

6. Using the inside circle of a masking tape roll (about 3" diameter), trace on railroad board or cardboard the round body shape of Rosie. Cut one circle per child. Using this same shape, trace and cut one wallpaper circle for each child.

7. On sentence strips print the text from *Rosie's Walk*. Cut these into phrases to match the book.

8. Using the text as a guide, make your own blackline of the word strips for this booklet. (Copyright prevents us from including the words.) See the picture under Extension for placement of the strips.

9. Cut triangular-shaped fox heads from light brown construction paper. The triangles should be 1½" on each side. Each child will need six of these for the booklet.

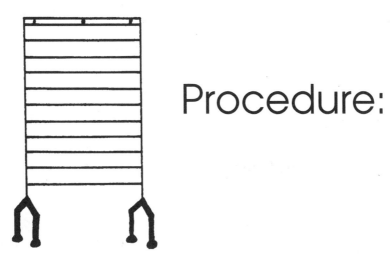

Procedure:

1. Help the children examine the cover of *Rosie's Walk*. Where does this story take place? Who do you think Rosie is? Where do you think she will go on her walk? What will she see?

2. Read *Rosie's Walk* by Pat Hutchins. While you are reading, discuss the pictures and have the children predict what will happen to the fox in each situation. Does Rosie know the fox is following her? Why not?

3. Develop the meaning of the language by helping the children dramatize each prepositional phrase. "Show me how you can you walk across something." (around something, past something, over something, etc.) This may be difficult for many five year-olds as they are confused by terms such as past, through and across.

4. Read the book again, using the my turn, your turn technique.

5. Using the small pictures from blacklines 21 and 22, help the children sequence the story in the pocket chart. Leave the top pocket open as you will add the first seven words at a later time in the lesson.

6. Place the phrase strips somewhere in the room so they may be easily seen and obtained by the children.

7. Using phonetic clues, the children match each phrase to the appropriate picture.

8. At this time the only remaining sentence strip is the one containing the first seven words of the story. Help the children read and decide where to place it.

9. Read or chant the entire story from the pocket chart.

10. Take the pictures out of the pocket chart and distribute these to the class. The children then match the pictures to the appropriate phrases.

11. Now take the phrase strips *and* the pictures out of the pocket chart and distribute these to the class. The children rebuild the entire story using both the picture cards and the sentence strips. Check for accuracy by using the book and then reread.

Extensions: *Rosie Booklet and Rewrites*

***Rosie's Walk* Booklet :** Following is an illustration of the booklet. The pictures are self-explanatory but a few notes may be helpful.

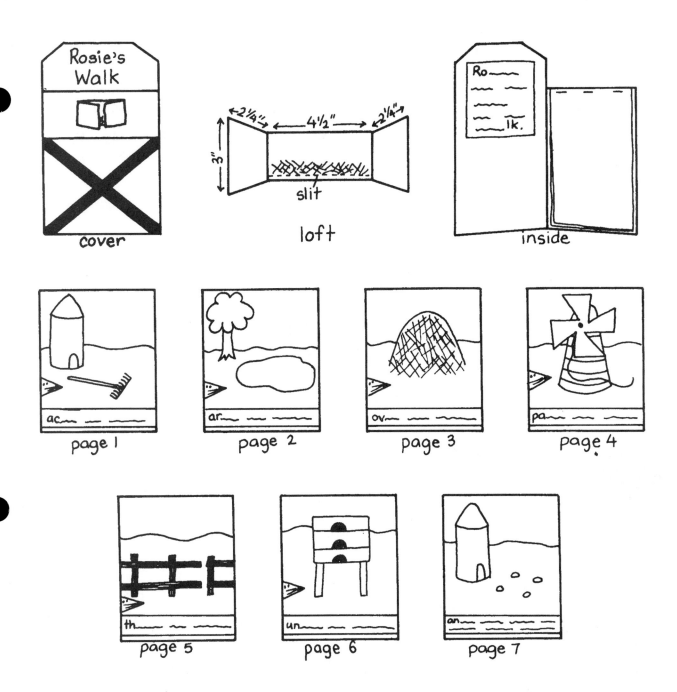

Cover: (This sounds much more complicated than it is!) Fold a piece of 12" x 18" red construction paper in half. Glue the yellow barn roof to the top of the front cover as shown in the illustration. The yellow roof will be about 2½" higher than the top of the red construction paper. We suggest that you pre-fold the black construction paper for the hayloft as it may be too difficult for the children. Draw a black line 7" from the bottom of the red construction paper. Glue the black strips that make an "x" for the door below this line and then glue the hayloft in place above the line. Glue down raffia or straw for hay. After the cover is completed, you will need to make a slit for Rosie to sit in her nest. Write the title, "Rosie's Walk" on the yellow roof. On the back of the front cover glue the first seven words to the story.

We would like to thank Sandra Won, a first grade teacher, for sharing her wonderful barn cover with us!

Page 1: All of the remaining pages will be on light blue construction paper. The children glue one of the silos down and illustrate the background, including a rake in yard. Add a nose and eyes to one of the triangle fox heads, as shown, and glue this down on the left hand edge of the page. Glue the words (from the blackline that you made) at the bottom of the page.

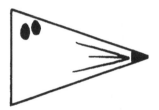

Page 2: The children cut a pond shape from the dark blue 9″ x 6″ construction paper. Glue this down. Add background, especially the wonderful tree that is depicted in the book. Add the fox and appropriate words.

Page 3: The children cut out the haystack and glue it down. Glue raffia or straw for the hay and illustrate the background. Finish with the fox and the appropriate words.

Page 4: The children cut out the two parts of the mill. Illustrate the background and glue the mill base down. Use a brad to attach the top portion. Attach a piece of string to the brad as shown in the illustration. Add the fox and the words.

Page 5: The children draw the background. Help the children glue the brown construction paper fence strips in place. Add the fox and words. When the glue is dry, the teacher cuts a slit about 3½" x ¼" for Rosie to go through.

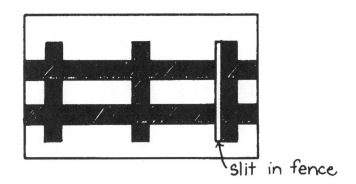

slit in fence

Page 6: The children cut the beehive out, illustrate the background and glue the beehive down. Be sure not to glue the legs of the bee-hive as Rosie will walk under them. Add the fox and words.

Page 7: The children cut the last silo out. Illustrate the background and glue the silo, fox and words. Add corn kernels for Rosie's dinner.

Rosie: The children glue the feet and beak to the cardboard circle. Add a feather for the tail. Glue a wallpaper circle on top of the cardboard circle. Glue a googly eye down.

cardboard

Rewrite: This may be done as a large group or individually with more mature children. Brainstorm for other creatures and their habitats. Discuss how that creature will move – crawl, slither, swim, gallop, etc. Also, if you wish, brainstorm for a predator for the creature. (fish/shark, mouse/cat, worm/bird, etc.) Once the creature and the predator have been decided upon, brainstorm for places this creature will go. The children then make a booklet similar to *Rosie's Walk.* Be sure to have available lots of art materials for the children to choose from. If this is a whole group activity the product will be a class book. The creature may be made into a finger puppet or merely attached to a popsicle stick. Here is an example from a kindergarten child:

Wanda the Worm

Wanda the Worm crawled and crawled
across the grass
around the tree
over the garden hose
past the bricks
through the flowers
under the leaves
and got back in time for her nap.

Activity 3

Chickens Aren't the Only Ones

Materials:

- *Flap Your Wings* by P. D. Eastman
- *Chickens Aren't The Only Ones* by Ruth Heller
- Set of animal picture cards
- 12" x 18" piece of railroad board for Oviparous class book cover
- Blackline 23 for book pages
- Blacklines 24–26 for pocket chart pictures
- Sixteen pieces of 4" x 5" tagboard to mount the above pictures
- Blackline 27 for the bulletin board eggs
- Colored pencils or crayons
- Laminating film or contact paper
- 12" x 18" white construction paper for the bulletin board eggs
- 9" x 12" white or manila construction paper for the class book
- Sentence strips

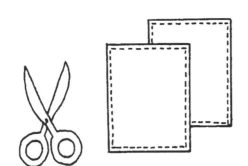

Preparation:

1. On sentence strips print *either A or B:*

A.

> A _____ hatches from an egg.

> An _____ hatches from an egg.

> But a _____ doesn't hatch from an egg.

> But an _____ doesn't hatch from an egg.

B.

> A _____ is oviparous.

> An _____ is oviparous.

> But a _____ isn't oviparous.

> But an _____ isn't oviparous.

2. When printing the following poem, omit the lines but leave enough space for the pictures from blacklines 24–26 to be inserted.

Although we have made every effort to locate the current copyright holder of the the poem, *Eggs,* we were unable to trace it. We will be happy to correct this omission.

Eggs

Lots of animals come from eggs _____
Some with fins ____ and some with legs ____
Some that chatter ____ and some that cheep ____
Some that fly ____ and some that creep ____
Some that slither ____ and some that run ____
Some with feathers ____ and some with none _____
Animal eggs can be quite small ____
Or just as big as a tennis ball ____
The animals here, they're quite a few _____
Hatch from eggs ____ and lay them too ____

3. Color blacklines 24–26. Cut apart, mount on tagboard cards and laminate or contact. Please read the description of the two extensions found at the end of this activity. One is for a bulletin board and the other is for a class book. After you decide which one you wish to do, prepare only for that activity.

Class Book:

4. Duplicate blackline 23, one per child, on white or manila construction paper.

5. For the front and back cover cut two eggs shapes (a little bit larger than the children's pages) from railroad board. Print *What is Oviparous?* on one of the egg shapes and then cut it apart in a zig-zag fashion. Laminate or contact all three pieces. Use strapping tape at the sides to connect the front and the back.

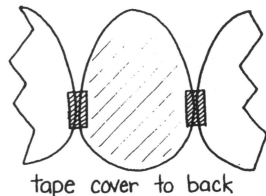

cover   tape cover to back

Bulletin Board:

6. Fold 12″ by 18″ white or manila construction paper in the following manner:

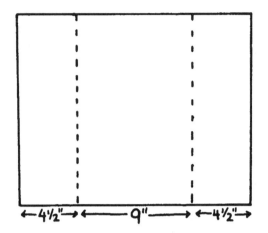 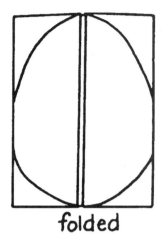

←4½″→ ←———9″———→ ←4½″→

folded

7. Use blackline 27 for a pattern and trace an egg on the folded papers for each child. Please note that the sides of the egg will not be cut off and that is the reason they are flat. They will open up when they are displayed on the bulletin board.

Procedure:

1. Put a book cover on *Flap Your Wings*. It is more fun if the children do not see the picture of Junior before hearing the story.
2. Read and enjoy the book *Flap Your Wings*. Ask the children if they can guess what animal will come out of the egg that the little boy found. They can look at the picture at the beginning of the story to predict.
3. Brainstorm orally for other animals that hatch from eggs.
4. At this point we like to involve the parents. We send the following

choral reading. Divide your class in half. The entire class reads the first and the last two lines. The remaining lines are read in an alternating style by the two sections.

Extensions: *Class Book and Bulletin Board*

Class Book: Distribute one copy of blackline 23 to each child. Help each child choose an animal picture to use as a reference when s/he illustrate his/her page for the class book. (Not only do the pictures give the children help with their drawings but they assure you a variety of animals in your book.) Children love to use colored pencils for this activity because they are able to put in much more detail than crayons allow. Depending on the children's ability, take dictation or have the children write **"A _____ is oviparous."** or **"A _____ hatches from an egg."** Staple the pages to the top of the back cover as shown in the illustration:

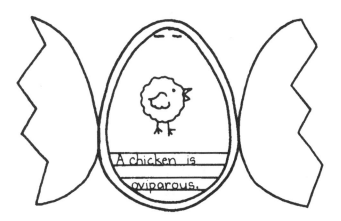

Read and enjoy this new book and add to your class library.

Bulletin Board: Distribute the folded paper with the egg shape tracing. The children cut out the egg shape, being careful not to cut the sides. Help each child choose an animal picture to use as a reference for their illustration on the inside of the egg.

On the outside of the egg the child prints the name of the animal.

On the inside the child draws the animal and prints the phrase *hatches from an egg* or *is oviparous*. Display on the bulletin board and read each one.

outside

inside

As an added treat we read *How Fletcher Was Hatched!* by Wende and Harry Devlin. We are told that this book is now out of print. Perhaps you can locate it in your school or public library or possibly know someone who is lucky enough to have a copy. This story is about a dog named Fletcher who has his nose bent out of shape and wants to get the attention of his mistress. His friends help build a huge egg around Fletcher and the fun begins.

Activity 4

Seven Eggs

Materials:

We suggest that you complete Activity 3 before using
***Seven Eggs* so the children will have a general background**
of animals that hatch from eggs.

- *Seven Eggs* by Meredith Hooper
- *The Golden Egg Book* by Margaret Wise Brown
- Blacklines 28–32 for the booklet
- Blacklines 33–34 for pocket chart pictures
- Seven pieces of 4" x 5" tagboard to mount pocket chart pictures
- Blackline 34 for the accordion booklet
- Blackline 35 for the pocket chart extension
- Four pieces of 5" x 6" tagboard to mount pocket chart pictures
- Sentence strips
- Felt pens
- Contact paper or laminating film
- 6" x 24" piece of construction or butcher paper, one per child
  (any light color will do) for the accordion booklet
- One bag of miniature chocolate eggs, one egg per child
- A factual book with photographs, illustrating an animal hatching
  from an egg
- White or manila construction paper for the booklet

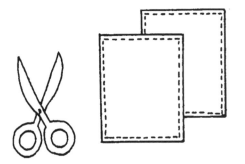

Preparation:

1. For the booklet duplicate blacklines (28–31), one per child, on yellow construction paper.

Please note that there are seven pictures for the pocket chart. We could only fit six to a page so number 7 is on Blackline 34.

2. Color, cut and mount the pocket chart pictures from blacklines 33 and 34. Contact or laminate.
3. Duplicate blackline 34, one per child, for the accordion book.
4. Fold the 6" x 24" construction paper into four equal parts, accordion style.

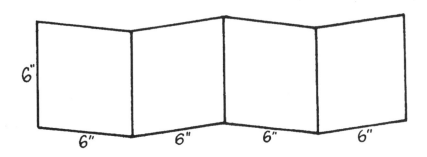

5. On sentence strips print the following:

On _____

the _____ egg

cracked

and out came

a baby_____.

6. On individual word cards print the names of the days of the week, the ordinal number names (first through seventh) and the animal names. (Refer to the book for the animals.)
7. Color, cut and mount the four pictures from blackline 35. Contact or laminate.
8. On sentence strips print the text from blackline 34.

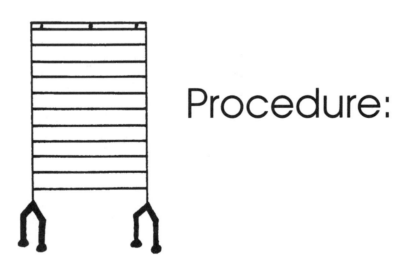

Procedure:

1. Begin reading *The Golden Egg Book* by Margaret Wise Brown. Stop at the bottom of the first page and help the children brainstorm for what might be inside this egg.

2. Continue reading and enjoy the humor and the wonderful ending.

3. Discuss what the children think it would be like to be inside an egg. How would you feel? How would your body look? How would you get out?

4. At this point, we like to read a factual book, with photographs, about hatching animals. The book we like to use (*What's Inside?*) is, unfortunately, out of print. We hope you will be able to locate this book, possibly at the library, or find another text that is similar in format.

5. Refer back to *The Golden Egg Book* and ask the children to pretend they are the little duckling, all curled up, inside the egg. The whole class dramatizes how the duckling would look, sound and finally, get out of the egg. How would you peck at the shell? How would you wiggle out of the shell? How would you try to stand? How would you stretch? What do you sound like? How do you feel? Are you scared? Etc.

6. Display the cover of *Seven Eggs.* Draw the children's attention to the number and the size of the eggs. Are all eggs the same size? Why not? What animals do you think might be in the large eggs? What animals do you think might be in the middle size eggs? How about the small eggs? Why do you think there are seven eggs?

7. Read and enjoy the entire book, predicting as you read each page.

8. After reading the book, look back at the pictures of the eggs and see if the children can remember which animal came out of each egg.

9. Using the pocket chart pictures from blacklines 33–34, help the children sequence the animals from the story. Be sure to place them to the far right of the pocket chart. Now, using phonetic clues, help the children match the animal names to the pictures and place these word cards directly to the left of each picture.

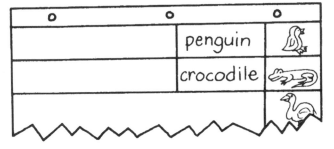

10. If your children are not familiar with the names of the days of the week, have them use your classroom calendar as a reference. Distribute the days of the week word cards to the class and add these to the far left of the animal names in the pocket chart.

Monday		penguin	
Tuesday		crocodile	
		ostrich	

11. This book offers a wonderful opportunity to work with ordinal numerals. Distribute the ordinal numeral word cards to the children. Using phonetic clues, help the children place the cards in the pocket chart in the correct order.

Monday	first	penguin	
Tuesday	second	crocodile	
Wednesday	third	ostrich	

12. Distribute the days of the week word cards to the children and let them practice reading them. Place them in the pocket chart in sequential order several times. (You may wish to use a song to help instill the correct sequence.)

13. Repeat step 12 using the ordinal numeral word cards.

14. Use the following structure for each line in the pocket chart and chant: "On _____ the ____ egg cracked and out came a baby _____" (This step is all oral.)

15. If you are lucky enough to have side-by-side pocket charts, leave the words and pictures alone. If you do not, remove them and place these words and pictures where they may easily be seen and obtained by the children.

16. Place the printed frame that was chanted (in step 14) in the pocket chart. Help the children build the first page of the story by placing the appropriate cards in the correct blanks. As each new page is developed, place the new cards on top of the previous ones.

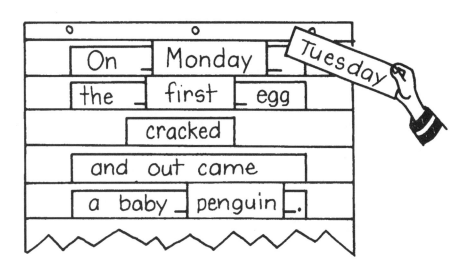

17. An idea we like is to fill an empty *L'eggs* container with small chocolate eggs and before opening it, ask the children what they think is inside **this** egg. Distribute the chocolate and enjoy!

Extensions:

Seven Eggs Booklet

We would like to thank a fellow teacher and good friend, Nancy Mullin, for the following idea.

1. Distribute the booklet pages from blacklines 28–31. The children color each animal.

2. Distribute the small eggs from blackline 32. Direct the children to find the egg that says *a penguin.* Cut that egg out.

3. Put paste or glue on the "X" space.

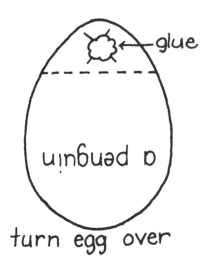

4. Turn the egg over and attach this small egg by matching the "X" on the small egg to the "X" on the booklet page above the penguin. Be sure the name of the animal is on the **inside** of the egg after it is glued down. The animal name will be read when the small egg is lifted. Also be careful not to glue the egg on top of the animal.

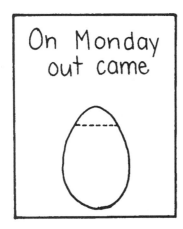 

5. Continue in the same manner until all of the pages have been completed.

6. The children sequence the pages of their booklets, staple, read and take home.

Accordion Booklet

1. Using the prepared sentence strips and pictures from blackline 35, develop in the pocket chart the four pages of the accordion booklet. Chant several times.

2. Distribute the pre-folded accordion booklets and a copy of blackline 34.

3. Help the children make the booklet as shown in the illustration. The easiest sequence to follow is to glue the words down, illustrate the background, glue the eggs down and lastly, draw the chicks.

Activity 5

The Chicken Book

Materials:

- *The Chicken Book* by Garth Williams
- Sentence strips
- Felt pens
- Contact or laminating film
- Green pipe cleaners, two 2″ pieces per child
- Brown pipe cleaners, two 2″ pieces per child
- Dried corn kernels, five per child (a pet food store has these)
- Small artificial leaves, three per child
- Small stones, three per child, (a store with aquarium items has these)
- Blacklines 36–37 for the pop-up booklet
- Blacklines 38–39 for the pocket chart
- Six pieces of 4″ x 5″ tagboard to mount the pocket chart pictures
- One piece of 8½″ x 11″ tagboard to mount blackline 39
- Blackline 40 for *Talking Chicks* book for the Extension
- 9″ x 12″ manila or white construction paper (seven pieces per child for the pop-up booklet)
- 9″ x 12″ white and yellow construction paper, one per child for the pop-up booklet characters
- Pre-inked stamp pad
- Black fine-tipped felt pens

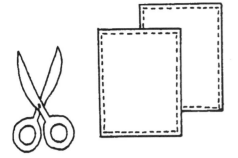

Preparation:

1. Duplicate blackline 36 on yellow construction paper, one per child.
2. Duplicate blackline 37 on white construction paper, one per child.
3. Make your own blackline of the words found in the text for the pop-up booklet. (Copyright prevents us from giving you the words.) Duplicate and cut apart.

Said the 〜 〜〜 〜〜 〜 〜 〜 〜〜 worm.	Said the 〜〜 〜 〜 〜 〜 〜 〜 〜 〜 〜 slug.
Said the 〜〜 〜〜 〜 〜 〜 〜 〜 〜 〜 〜 meal.	Said the 〜 〜 〜 〜 〜 〜 〜 〜 〜 leaf.
Said the 〜 〜〜 〜 〜 〜 〜 〜 〜 〜 〜 stone.	Now see 〜 〜 〜 〜 〜 〜 〜 SCRATCH!

4. Color, cut and mount blackline 38 for the pocket chart activities. Contact or laminate.
5. Mount blackline 39 on an 8½" x 11" piece of tagboard. Cut apart and contact or laminate.
6. If you would like, you can create a big book using your copy of *The Chicken Book*. Enlarge the words of this poem by printing them on 1½" wide sentence strips and glue the strips over the original text. This way the entire class will be able to see the words.
7. You will need to prepare the blank pop-up booklets beforehand. Some teachers feel the children are capable of folding and cutting their own, but we have found it a difficult, if not impossible, task for a young child.

For each child, fold three pieces of 9″ x 12″ manila construction paper in half. Cut two 2″ cuts on the *left* hand side of the fold as shown in the illustration.

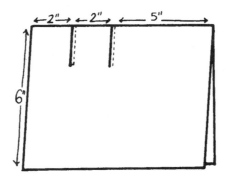

Fold three more pieces of 9″ x 12″ manila construction paper in half. Cut two 2″ cuts on the *right* hand side of the fold as shown in the illustration.

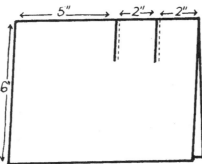

Fold one piece of 9″ x 12″ manila construction paper in half. This piece will be the cover and it will not have any cuts.

To prepare each page, you will need to carefully poke that 2″ section that you cut *toward the inside* of the fold, refolding that 2″ section as shown in the illustration.

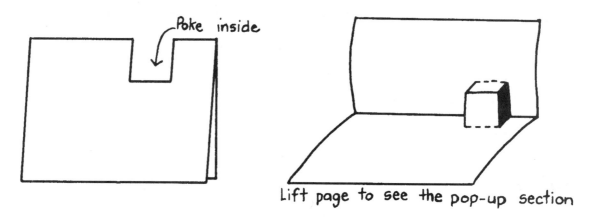

Lift page to see the pop-up section

42

After each of the six pages have been prepared, assemble the booklet as follows:

Open up the folded cover and lay it flat.
For page 1, place a left sided pop-up page directly on top of the cover. Glue or staple in the four corners of the *top* half.

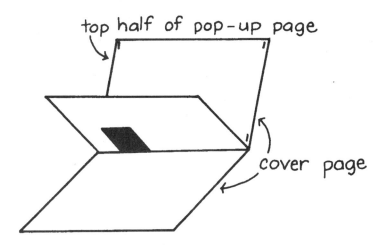

Use a right sided pop-up page next. Attach the back of the *bottom* half of page 1 to the back of the *top* half of page 2.

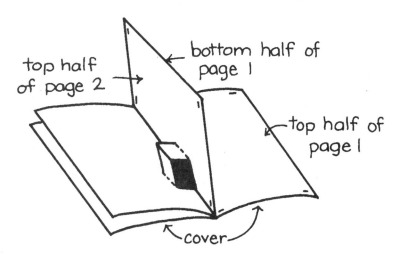

To finish the booklet, continue in the same manner, alternating right and left-sided pop-ups. Attach the bottom cover to the back of the bottom of the last pop-up page.

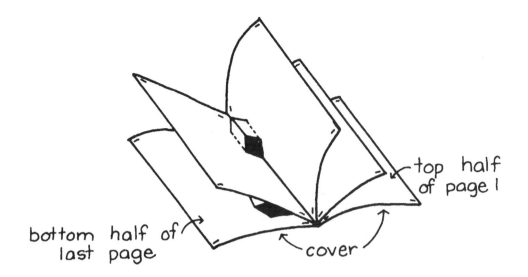

bottom half of last page

top half of page 1

cover

8. Cut the pipe cleaners into 2″ pieces.

9. Copy the following structure on sentence strips:
   (Do not cut the words apart.)

   Said the ___ little chick with _____,
   I wish I could find _____.

10. Referring to the book, print the remaining phrases (there should be ten in all) on sentence strips. Do not cut these into individual word cards! It is not necessary to print the ordinal numbers as they are found on blackline 39.

11. Copy the last verse (where the Mother Hen is speaking) on sentence strips. (Do not cut these words apart.)

12. Duplicate blackline 40 for the *Talking Chicks* Book (class book). Cut into fourths. Each child will need one talking bubble.

Procedure:

1. Before reading this book, brainstorm for what the children know about chickens. What do they look like? What is a female chicken called? What is a male chicken called? What do chickens eat? (Show the cover of the book at this time and identify the various things the chicks are eating.) What sounds do baby chicks make? (roosters? hens?) Etc.

2. Read and enjoy *The Chicken Book.* (If you made a big book, track as you read.) Help the children predict which chick will be next (second, third, etc.) and what each chick would like to find to eat. Discuss the humor in the pictures. Why can't the chicks see the food?

3. Read the book again, using the my turn, your turn technique. *If you used Activity 4, **Seven Eggs,** the children will be familiar with the ordinal numerals. If you did not, you may need to spend some additional time developing this concept.*

4. Distribute the ordinal numeral word cards to the children. Using phonetic clues, help the children place the cards in the pocket chart in the correct order.

5. Discuss the shortened version of ordinal numerals (1st, 2nd, 3rd, 4th and 5th). Help the children understand how these are like the written words. Distribute these numeral cards to the children and help them place them in the pocket chart next to the appropriate word cards.

6. Distribute the pocket chart pictures, blackline 38. Using the book as a guide, help the children sequence the pictures next to the ordinal numerals in the pocket chart.

7. Read the book again. Find all the rhyming words and discuss.

8. Place all the picture and ordinal numeral cards at the very bottom of the pocket chart. At the top of the pocket chart, place the printed structure that you made in step 9 under Preparation. The ten phrase cards should be placed so that they may easily be seen and obtained by the children.

9. Working with the structure, help the children build the first verse by placing the appropriate cards in the correct blanks. Read together. As each new verse is developed, place the new phrase cards on top of the previous ones and read again. Place the last verse in the pocket chart and read together.

10. This poem offers a wonderful opportunity for language development. Discuss the following phrases and how they could be dramatized: a queer little squirm, an odd little shrug, a sharp little squeal, a small sigh of grief and a faint little moan.

11. Divide your class into five groups. If you have a strong reader, assign her the mother hen's part. If not, the teacher takes that part.

12. Referring to the book, dramatize the entire poem, having each group read and act out their part. Another way to use this poem is to have the entire class read and act out all the parts.

Extensions: *The Chicken Book and Talking Chicks Class Book*

The Chicken Book: This booklet will take several days to complete. Each child will need an empty pop-up book, two mother hens, the booklet title, three chicks facing left, two chicks facing right, pre-cut words, two pieces of 2" green pipe cleaner, two pieces of 2" brown pipe cleaner, five kernels of corn, three artificial leaves and three small stones. *The reason the children need so many items is that the last page of the booklet will contain one of each of these items.*

For each page, the children will need to illustrate a background, using crayons. Make sure the children color before they glue the chicks down.

Color the feet and beaks of the five chicks and the combs and beaks of the mother hens. Cut these out. Glue the chicks facing left to the pages that have the pop-up sections on the left hand side. Reverse this for the chicks facing right. The chicks' feet should appear to be standing on the fold and be centered so the chicks do not hang out the side of the booklet. Glue the appropriate food item in back of each chick. Glue the words to the bottom of the page.

The last page includes the mother hen and one of each food item.

The Talking Chicks Class Book: On the chalkboard print
"I want _____." Brainstorm for things chickens like to
eat (bugs, crumbs, seeds, etc.), Illustrate and label each item
that the children name. After the brainstorming, chant or read
each suggestion using the frame. (I want a caterpillar. I want a
dragonfly. I want...)

Distribute the small book pages, one per child. Using a stamp pad,
each child makes one thumbprint in the lower left hand corner of

the page. The child uses a black fine-
tipped felt pen to illustrate a beak, feet,
eyes and wings. Using crayons, each
child draws what their chick wants to
eat and then colors in a background.
Using the chalkboard as a guide, the
child copies the frame and the name of
the food into the talking bubble.

Add a cover of your choice and bind together into a class book and
read. Add to your class library.

Note: some children may enjoy making several pages and
creating their own individual booklets.

Activity 6

Humpty Dumpty

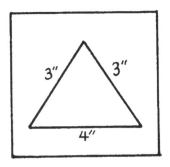

Materials:

- Blackline 75 for the pocket chart pictures
- Five pieces of 4" x 5" tagboard for mounting the pocket chart pictures
- Blacklines 41–43 for the booklet
- Blacklines 45–48 for the *make a play*
- Various colors of construction paper for the booklet and play
- Felt pens
- Contact paper or laminating film
- Sentence strips
- 3" x 3" purple construction paper, one per child, for booklet
- Purple construction paper triangle, one per child, for booklet. Cut the triangles so they measure about 3" x 3" x 4".

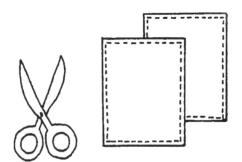

Preparation:

1. Color, cut and mount the pocket chart pictures from blackline 75. Contact or laminate. Print the words to *Humpty Dumpty,* using five sentence strips, as shown on blackline 41. Make another set, but cut this set into individual word cards.

2. Duplicate blackline 41 (words to the rhyme), one per child, on white paper. You may wish to either cut these apart into sentence strips or have the children cut them as they make the booklet.

3. Duplicate blackline 42 (cover for booklet), one per child, on white construction paper.

4. Duplicate blackline 43 (egg shapes), one per child, on white construction paper.

5. Duplicate blackline 44 (horse shapes) on brown construction paper. Each child needs one large and one small oval shape.

6. Each child will need five pages of yellow construction paper and a copy of the cover for this booklet. You may wish to staple this booklet ahead of time for kindergarten children. Older children are able to sequence the pages themselves and staple.

7. Duplicate blackline 45 (castle), one per child, on grey construction paper.

8. Duplicate blackline 46 (Humpty), one per child, on white construction paper.

9. Duplicate blackline 47 (horse and man), one per child, on white or manila construction paper.

10. Duplicate blackline 48 (brick wall), on red construction paper. Cut in half as there are two walls on this page. Each child will need one wall.

11. Fold in half any dark color of 12″ x 18″ construction paper so it measures 9″ x 12″, one per child. (This is the cover for the play.)

12. On a sentence strip, write the numerals 1–5 and cut apart.

Procedure:

1. Introduce this rhyme by chanting the words. Invite the children to join in. Repeat several times. (The children should have this rhyme memorized before working with it in the pocket chart.)

2. Chant the rhyme using patchem. (The children clap and pat their laps to the meter of the rhyme.)

3. To help develop meaning, we like to dramatize this rhyme at this point. Ask the children: What is Humpty Dumpty? What is a great fall? What are the king's horses and the king's men? Why couldn't they put him together again?

4. Divide the class into three parts: Humpty Dumpty, king's horses and king's men. Chant the rhyme again as all the parts are dramatized. You may wish to repeat this two more times so that each child has a turn with each part.

5. Ask the children what they think Humpty Dumpty might have been doing on the wall to cause him to fall. We have gotten very creative answers in the past (break dancing!). You may wish to have the class dramatize these ideas as they are mentioned.

6. Place the numerals 1–5 vertically in the pocket chart. Chant the rhyme again, adding the pocket chart pictures as you go.

7. Distribute the picture cards to five children and have the class help sequence them in the pocket chart.

8. Take the numerals out of the pocket chart, leaving the pictures. Ask the children to hide their eyes while you mix up the order of the pictures. Distribute the five numeral cards to the class and help the children match them to the scrambled pictures.
   (**Note**: this technique was presented to us by Marlene and Bob McCracken.) It is a very effective procedure, but more difficult than you might assume.

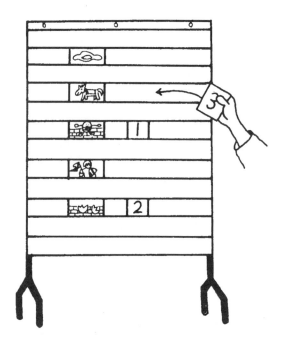

9. Remove the numerals and pictures from the pocket chart.
   Note: you have two sets of words for this rhyme; one set is line-by-line and the other set is made up of individual words. Begin by placing the line-by-line set of words in the pocket chart. Chant or read, tracking with your hand as you develop each line.

10. Distribute the individual words of the first line to the children. Help the children match these words to those in the pocket chart. (Place them directly on top of the matching word.) Continue in the same manner until the entire rhyme has been developed. Read line-by-line.

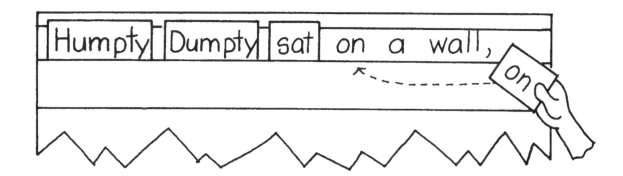

11. Remove everything from the pocket chart. Distribute only picture and individual word cards and help the children rebuild the entire rhyme in the pocket chart. Chant and read together.

 **Extensions:** *Humpty Dumpty booklet and Make a Play*

(Both of these activities will take several days to complete.)

Humpty Dumpty Booklet: *We would like to thank Patti Ferroni, a creative first grade teacher, for this delightful booklet idea.*

Before beginning this booklet, use individual chalkboards and practice drawing happy and sad faces for Humpty Dumpty.

Cover: the children use crayons to color the cover (blackline 42).

Page 1: Children glue the appropriate sentence strip to the bottom of a piece of yellow construction paper. Illustrate a wall and grass. The children cut the undivided oval from blackline 43 and add a crayon face and belt. Glue this to the top of the wall. Add legs and arms with crayon.

53

Page 2: Glue the sentence strip to the bottom of a piece of yellow construction paper. Illustrate the grass. Use one of the divided ovals from blackline 43 and add a crayon belt and sad face. Cut the oval apart on the lines and carefully glue this down (as shown in the illustration). Add arms and legs with crayons.

Page 3: Glue the words down on a piece of yellow construction paper. Illustrate the grass. Each child needs one large and one small oval (blackline 44) that was duplicated on brown construction paper for the horse. Glue the ovals in place and add legs, tail and features with crayon.

Page 4: Glue the words down on a piece of yellow construction paper. Help the children draw a large U shape on the page. You may need to draw this shape for younger children as they might not be able to make it large enough. Draw eyes, nose, mouth and ears with crayons.

Glue the purple construction paper (3″ x 3″ square and the 3″ x 3″ x 4″ triangle) to the yellow construction paper to make the hat. Add hair with crayons.

Page 5: Glue the words down on a piece of yellow construction paper. Illustrate the grass with a crayon. Use the remaining divided oval from blackline 43 and illustrate a face and belt. Cut the oval apart and carefully glue the three pieces at random on the grass.

Make a Play: *We would like to thank Wendy Leibrandt, a good friend and fellow teacher, for sharing this fantastic play with us.*

Begin with the castle. This will not only be the backdrop but also be used as a storage area for all the characters of this play. Outline or color the features of the grey castle that was made from blackline 45. Cut the castle. Open up the large 12″ x 18″ construction paper folder. (If you open the folder, the children are less apt to try to glue the castle upside down!) Carefully glue around the sides and bottom of the castle, being sure not to glue the top. Glue the castle to the paper folder, matching the corners at the bottom. You have now created a storage pocket.

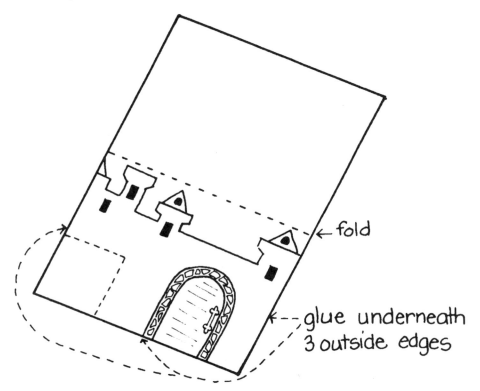

← fold

←-- glue underneath
3 outside edges

55

Use a black crayon to color alternating bricks on the red construction paper wall. Carefully fold the wall on the dotted lines. Stand the castle up and glue the back section of the wall to the castle as shown in the illustration. Be sure that the wall ledge is somewhat even after it is glued as Humpty needs to sit on it.

glue back of wall onto castle

Color and cut Humpty Dumpty that was duplicated from blackline 46. Carefully fold on the dotted lines. Bring the top of the heads together and staple or glue.

Color the king's man and the horse. Cut out the rectangles and fold so they will stand up. Be sure to tell your children **not to cut** the individual horse and man as they do not stand as well as the larger rectangles.

When completed, set Humpty Dumpty on the ledge of the wall, place the king's man and the horse behind the castle and you are ready to make a play. Have the children chant the rhyme using the characters to dramatize the action.

This is a perfect lesson for bringing in factual information about
eggs. We like to use various math and science activities from AIMS.
If you are interested, you can get information from:
Aims Education Foundation, P.O. Box 7766, Fresno, CA 93747.

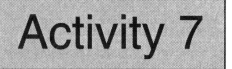

Activity 7

Hattie and the Fox

Materials:

- *Hattie and the Fox* by Mem Fox
- Blacklines 49–50 for the pocket chart
- Twelve pieces of 4″ x 5″ tagboard for mounting pocket chart pictures
- Sentence strips
- Felt pens
- Contact paper or laminating paper
- Construction paper or chart paper for the rewrite

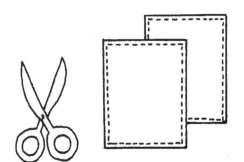

Preparation:

1. Color, cut and mount blacklines 49–50. Contact or laminate. We suggest making a felt pen border around each of the boxes on blackline 49, using a different color for each box. (This will help with matching the sentences to the correct animal.)

2. On sentence strips print the following:
   – the six things Hattie sees, beginning with the words
     "Goodness gracious me! I can see..."
   – the repetitive sentences of each of the five animals
     (**"Good grief!"said the goose.**) These sentences need to be
     printed in colors corresponding to those colors used on the
     borders of the pocket chart pictures on blackline 49.
3. Cut the above five sentence strips before the word *said.*
   This will create ten phrase cards.

Procedure:

1. Read and enjoy *Hattie and the Fox.* Encourage the children
   to join in on the repetitive sentences of the animals.
2. The teacher places the ten phrase cards in the pocket chart,
   creating the repetitive sentences of the five animals.
3. Read the book again, referring to the pocket chart as you
   come to the repetitive sentences. Track each sentence while
   the children chant or read.

4. Divide the class into five groups: a pig group, a goose group, a sheep group, a horse group and a cow group. Read the book again. The teacher reads the part of Hattie while each group joins in with their repeated sentence at the appropriate time.

5. Distribute the five animal pictures (not Hattie) to the class and help the children match them to the correct sentence.
   (**Note:** the pictures and the sentences are color-coded to help even the non-reader.) Read.

6. Distribute the five animal pictures and the ten phrase cards to the class. The children find their partners (making a group of three) and each group reads and places their sentences in sequence in the pocket chart.

7. Read the story again, asking the children to listen for all the parts of the fox that Hattie saw.

8. Ask the children to tell you what Hattie saw first. (a nose) Place that picture card (blackline 50) in the pocket chart. Continue in this manner until the entire fox is seen.

9. In the pocket chart, build Hattie's repetitive sentences, beginning with **"Goodness gracious me!"** Refer to the already sequenced pictures for accuracy. Read or chant.

10. This is a perfect time for drama. All the children act out all the parts as the teacher tells the story.

Extension: *Rewrite Class Book*

Before beginning this rewrite, you need to decide on a setting. After you have determined this, the children will brainstorm for a predator and the appropriate characters. From the brainstorming the children can decide on the final characters for this rewrite. Brainstorm for different comments for each of the characters to say. Also brainstorm for what parts of the predator the main character will see. You may wish to illustrate these on the chalkboard.

To make a *big book* of this extension activity, the teacher prints the text on large construction paper. The children illustrate. Tissue paper overlay, like the book, would be a wonderful medium, but a bit difficult for five year olds. The children prepare the artwork on separate pages and the teacher cuts it out and glues it with the appropriate text. Bind the pages into a book.

To make a *chart story* of this extension, the teacher prints the text on chart paper instead of construction paper. The children illustrate and the teacher glues the pictures down.

Suggested settings: a backyard or farm setting with a cat as the predator. The animals might include a mouse, a chick, a bird, a bunny and a puppy.

- an ocean setting with a shark as the predator
- a prehistoric setting with Tyrannosaurus Rex as the predator
- a forest setting with a bear as the predator

Activity 8

Too Many Eggs

Materials:

- *Too Many Eggs* by M. Christina Butler
- Sentence strips
- Felt pens
- Blacklines 51–54 for the booklet
- Blacklines 55–56 for the pocket chart
- Eight pieces of 4" x 5" tagboard for mounting the pocket chart pictures
- Contact paper or laminating film
- Uncooked spaghetti (sticks) for booklet
- 6" x 9" manila or light colored construction paper for the booklet pages, nine pages per child.

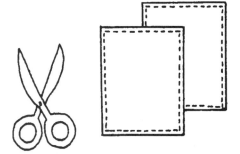

Preparation:

Although we have made every effort to locate the current copyright holder of the poem *Eggs In A Nest,* we were unable to trace it. We will be happy to correct this omission.

1. Follow the directions found on the inside cover of *Too Many Eggs* for the preparation before reading this book to your class.

   "Eggs In A Nest" makes a wonderful booklet to use as an extension. However, there are a significant number of unrelated words which may make it a bit difficult for five year olds. You may wish to create a shortened booklet version by using only the pages that refer to the numerals (blackline 51), the appropriate sentence strips (blackline 54) and five nests (blackline 53).

2. For the *complete* booklet, follow the remaining steps. Duplicate blacklines 51–52 on white construction paper, one set per child, for the booklet.

3. Duplicate blackline 53 on brown construction paper. Each child will need nine nests for the booklet.

4. Duplicate blackline 54, one page per child, for the booklet.

5. Color, cut and mount blacklines 55–56 for the pocket chart. After contacting or laminating, you may wish to glue uncooked spaghetti to one of the nests to resemble sticks.

6. Print the poem, *Eggs In A Nest* on sentence strips. To help the children with the pocket chart activities, we suggest you print the text, using the following color coding:

red   Eggs in a nest – 1, 2, 3
            Mother Hen keeps them warm as can be.

green   Eggs in a nest – 4, 5, 6
            Lie in a bed made of sticks.

blue   Eggs in a nest – 7, 8, 9
            Start to hatch in the bright sunshine.

brown   Eggs in a nest – 10 I see,
            Soon little chickies they will be.

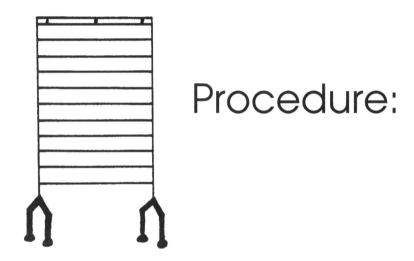

Procedure:

1. Discuss the cover of *Too Many Eggs*, being sure to name the animals and the reason for so many eggs.
2. Read this delightful book, having the children participate as indicated. The children will find it very humorous that Mrs. Bear could not count – and that they can! Your class will probably want you to read this book more than once!
3. Discuss what using too much of one thing might do. (mustard on a hotdog, salt on scrambled eggs, salad dressing on salad, etc.) Did too many eggs ruin Mrs. Bear's cake? Why not?
4. Tell the children you have a poem about eggs. Introduce the poem *Eggs In A Nest* in the pocket chart using only the pictures from blacklines 55–56. Place the pictures in the pocket chart, one at a time, as you chant the poem.

5. Divide your class into two groups, with each group chanting alternating lines.

"Mother Hen keeps them warm as can be."

Group 1

Group 2

6. Chant several times, until the class has memorized the poem.
7. Add the color coded sentence strips, one at a time, as the children chant the poem.
8. For the older children, distribute all the sentence strips and the pictures and help the children rebuild the complete poem in the pocket chart.

Extension:

Eggs In A Nest booklet

(this will take several days to complete)

For **a shortened version,** refer back to step 1 under Preparation.

1. To make the *complete* booklet, each child will need the following:
   – nine pieces of 6″ x 9″ construction paper, any light color
   – nine brown nests
   – one copy of blackline 51
   – one copy of blackline 52
   – one copy of blackline 54 for the sentence strips
   – one piece of uncooked spaghetti, broken into pieces

2. The cover: add crayon highlights to the brown construction paper nest. Glue the nest and the title, *Eggs In A Nest* to a piece of 6″ x 9″ construction paper. Glue the group of eight eggs (labeled 'cover') to the center of the nest. Use crayons to illustrate grass.

cover

3. For each additional page, highlight the nest with crayons and glue it down on the construction paper. Add the appropriate sentence strips, the eggs and crayon detail as shown in the following illustration.

   Note: page 3 has spaghetti sticks added to the empty nest and page 5 has an illustrated sun.

Eggs in a nest – 1, 2, 3
page 1

Mother Hen keeps them warm as can be.
page 2

Eggs in a nest – 4,5,6
page 3

Lie in a bed made of sticks
page 4

Eggs in a nest – 7, 8, 9
page 5

Start to hatch in the bright sunshine.
page 6

Eggs in a nest – 10 I see
page 7

Soon little chickies they will be.
page 8

Activity 9

Across The Stream

Materials:

- *Across The Stream* by Mirra Ginsburg
- Domesticated Birds from *Farm Animals* by Pat Perea (*Come With Me* Science Series) or other factual information about chickens
- Blacklines 57 for the booklet cover
- Blackline 58 for the blank booklet pages
- Sentence strips for a strip booklet
- Felt pens
- 6″ x 4½″ yellow construction paper, one per child, for the back cover of the booklet

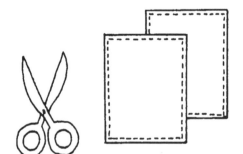
Preparation:

1. Duplicate blackline 57 on yellow construction paper. Cut these papers into fourths. Each child needs only one chick.
2. Duplicate blackline 58 on white ditto paper, 4–8 chick outlines per child. Cut these papers into fourths.

3. To prepare the strip booklet, fold the sentence strips in half and bind with a rubber band. Print **Chickens . . .** on the cover.

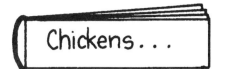

Procedure:

1. Read and enjoy *Across The Stream*, stopping periodically to help the children predict what a hen's bad dream might be, how the hen and her chicks will get across the stream, what happened to the bad dream, etc.

2. Begin a discussion about what the children know about chickens. Brainstorm on the chalkboard for **all** the ideas the children suggest. (Do not censor or make judgement calls at this time)

3. Chant all the ideas that were brainstormed beginning with *Chickens _____*.

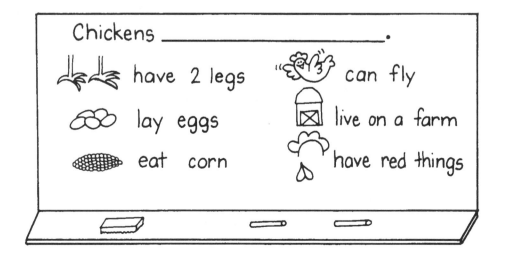

4. Present factual information, either from the *Come With Me* Science Series or from your own library. (The address for *Come With Me* is: S/S Publishing Co., Rt. 1, Box 0180, Shingle Springs, CA 95682) We like to start this part of the lesson by asking the children to listen carefully for all the things you can remember about a chicken. You may even have to give the children an idea of what to listen for – what they eat, what they look like, etc.

5. At this point return to the brainstorming on the chalkboard and check for accuracy and any omissions. This is where we help the children discover any misconceptions they have (for example, that chickens can fly).

6. Chant the new information.

7. Now record one fact on each page of the prepared strip book. **Note:** folding 8–10 sentence strips will give you 16–20 pages.

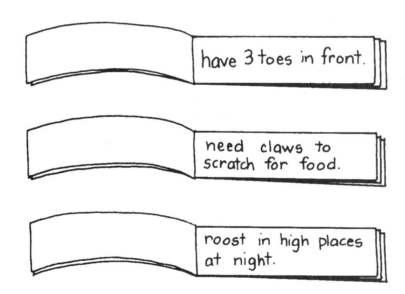

8. Read this *instant book* and add it to your class library.

Extension 1: *Me Too Booklet*

1. On the far left-hand side of the chalkboard print the following frames:

   I am _____.
   I have _____.
   I can _____.

2. Brainstorm on the chalkboard for likenesses and differences between a duckling and a chick.

   Note: You will have one list for *same* and two lists for *different*.

   Same:
   * yellow
   I am ____. * 2 feet
   I can ____. * an orange beak
   I have ____. * 2 wings
   * 2 eyes
   * eat worms
   * feathers
   * small

   Different:
   * webbed feet   * short beak
   * long beak   * scratch
   * say quack   * say cheep
   * waddle
   * swim

3. Using these frames, the children need to orally create many sentences that the duckling could say, and to which the chick could respond, "Me too!" As the children chant the sentences they have

just created they also need to chant the chick's response, *Me too!*
Note: Use only the brainstorming of the similarities at this point.

"I am yellow." "Me too!"
"I have an orange beak." "Me too!"
"I have feathers." "Me too!"
"I have two feet."   "Me too!"
"I can eat worms."   "Me too!"
  etc.

4. Now, using the brainstorming for differences, the children use the frames to orally create several sentences the duckling could say to which the chick would respond, *Not me!* Again the children will chant the ducklings's sentences and the chick's response, *Not me!*

"I can say quack."   "Not me!"
"I can swim." "Not me!"
"I can waddle." "Not me!"
"I have a long beak." "Not me!"
"I have webbed feet."   "Not me!"
  etc.

5. Before beginning the booklet, print **Me too!** and **Not me!** on the chalkboard. Distribute 4–6 booklet pages, blackline 57, to each child. For each page, except the last one, the children choose one sentence from the column labeled *same* for the duckling to say. Using the brainstorming as a guide, the children print this sentence inside the duckling's talking bubble and **Me too!** inside the chick's talking bubble. Color the pictures.

6. For the last page, the children choose one sentence from the duckling's column labeled "different" for the duckling to say. Referring to the brainstorming, the children print this sentence inside the duckling's talking bubble and **Not me!** inside the chick's talking bubble. Color the pictures.

last page

7. Distribute the cover (blackline 60) to the children. They only need to color the chick, print "Me too!" inside the talking bubble and sign their name. The children collate the pages and staple. Read to a friend.

Extension 2: Me Too! *by Mercer Mayer*

Read and enjoy the book, *Me Too!* This is a perfect conclusion to this lesson as the little sister, just like the chick, says "me too" until the very end.

Activity 11

Where's the Egg?

Materials:

Note: This final activity is only to be used if you are doing this theme at Easter time.

- *Where's My Easter Egg?* by Harriet Ziefert
- Blacklines 62–72 for the booklet
- Blacklines 73–74 for the pocket chart
- Seven pieces of 5" x 6" tagboard for mounting the pocket chart pictures
- Sentence strips
- Felt pens
- Contact paper or laminating film
- 4" x ¼" black construction paper strips for the whiskers, four per child
- 3" x 3" blue construction paper for the eyes, two per child
- 1" square pink construction paper for the nose, two per child
- Stickers: each child will need four small animal stickers and one Easter egg sticker.

Help the children dramatize *in, behind, over, under,* and *next to* various things in the room.

5. Read a third time using the my turn, your turn technique.
6. Using the pocket chart pictures from blacklines 73–74, help the children sequence the story.
7. Distribute the pictures and have the children sequence the story again, referring to the book to check for accuracy.
8. Place the sentence strips next to the appropriate pictures and read or chant each line as it is added.
9. Read the entire story from the pocket chart.
10. Distribute all pictures and sentence strips and tell the children to find their partners and rebuild the story in the pocket chart. Read to check for accuracy.

 Extension: *Where's The Egg? Booklet*

This booklet will take several days to complete. The children make their booklets in the same manner that yours was made. The directions are under Preparation.

Read *Where's My Easter Egg?* as a culminating activity, predicting what Nicky will find behind each flap. Discuss the similarities and differences in this book and *Where's The Egg?* You might wish to have an Easter egg hunt at this time. If you are doing this indoors and are anxious about not finding all the eggs, you can use stickers that may be traded in for real eggs at the end of the hunt.

Bibliography

Although we have made every effort to locate the current copyright holders of the materials used in this theme book, some we were unable to trace. We will be happy to correct any errors or omissions.

Brown, Margaret Wise, *The Golden Egg Book*, A Golden Book, Western Publishing Company, Inc., New York, NY, 1975.

Butler, M. Christina, *Too Many Eggs*, David R. Godine, Publisher, Inc., Boston, MA, 1988.

Casey, Patricia, *Cluck Cluck*, Lothrop, Lee & Shepard Books, New York, NY, 1988

Devlin, Wende and Harry, *How Fletcher Was Hatched!*, Parents' Magazine Press, New York, NY, 1969.

Eastman, P. D., *Flap Your Wings*, Random House, Inc., New York, NY, 1977.

Emberley, Ed, *Ed Emberley's Drawing Bokf of Animals*, Little, Brown and Company, Boston, MA, 1970.

Fox, Mem, *Hattie and the Fox*, Bradbury Press, New York, NY, 1987.

Galdone, Paul, *Henny Penny*, Scholastic Inc., New York, NY, 1968

Galdone, Paul, *The Little Red Hen*, Clarion Books, Ticknor & Fields: A Houghton Mifflin Company, New York, NY, 1973.

Ginsburg, Mirra, *Across The Stream*, Greenwillow Books, New York, NY, 1982.

Ginsburg, Mirra, *Good Morning, Chick*, Scholastic Inc., New York, NY, 1980.

Ginsburg, Mirra, *The Chick and the Duckling*, Macmillan Publishing Co., Inc., New York, NY, 1972.

Heller, Ruth, *Chickens Aren't The Only Ones*, Grosset & Dunlap, New York, NY, 1982.

Hill, Eric, *Spot's First Easter*, G. P. Putnam's Sons, New York, NY, 1988.

Hooper, Meredith, *Seven Eggs*, Harper & Row, Publishers, New York, NY, 1985.

Hutchins, Pat, *Rosie's Walk*, Scholastic Inc., New York, NY, 1987.

Kasza, Keiko, *The Wolf's Chicken Stew*, G. P. Putnam's Sons, New York, NY, 1987.

Kellogg, Steven, *Chicken Little*, Mulberry Books, New York, NY, 1987.

Mayer, Mercer, *Me Too!*, Golden Press, New York, NY, 1983.

McGovern, Ann, *Eggs On Your Nose*, Macmillan Publishing Company, New York, NY, 1987

Oppenheim, Joanne, *"Not Now!" Said the Cow*, A Bantam Little Rooster Book, New York, NY, 1989.

Seuss, Dr., *Green Eggs and Ham*, Beginner Books, Inc., New York, NY, 1960.

Willians, Garth, *The Chicken Book*, Doubleday Publishers, New York, NY, 1990.

Ziefert, Harriet, *The Prince's Tooth Is Loose*, A Random House Pictureback Reader, Random House, New York, NY, 1990.

Ziefert, Harriet, *Where's My Easter Egg?*, Viking Penguin Inc., New York, NY, 1985.

Available from Teaching Resource Center, P.O. Box 1509, San Leandro, CA 94577:

Little Red Hen Big Book, student-sized book and pocket chart strips.

Blacklines

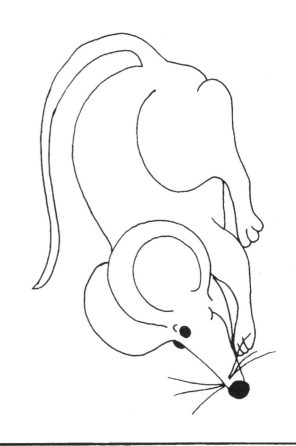

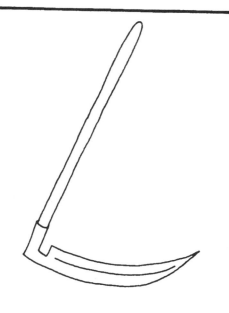

Little Red Hen_____the wheat.

_____

Little Red Hen_____the wheat.

Little Red Hen_____the treat.

_____

Little Red Hen_____the treat.

plants	waters	plants	waters
cuts	grinds	cuts	grinds
makes	eats	makes	eats

plants	waters	plants	waters
cuts	grinds	cuts	grinds
makes	eats	makes	eats

The
Little
Red Hen

by _____

7

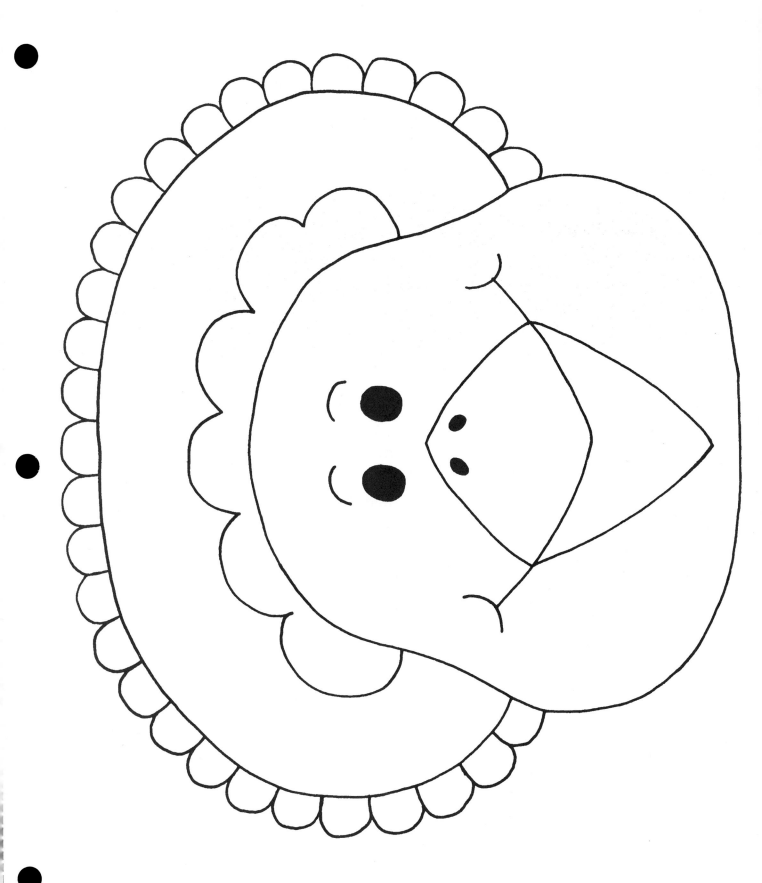

8

10

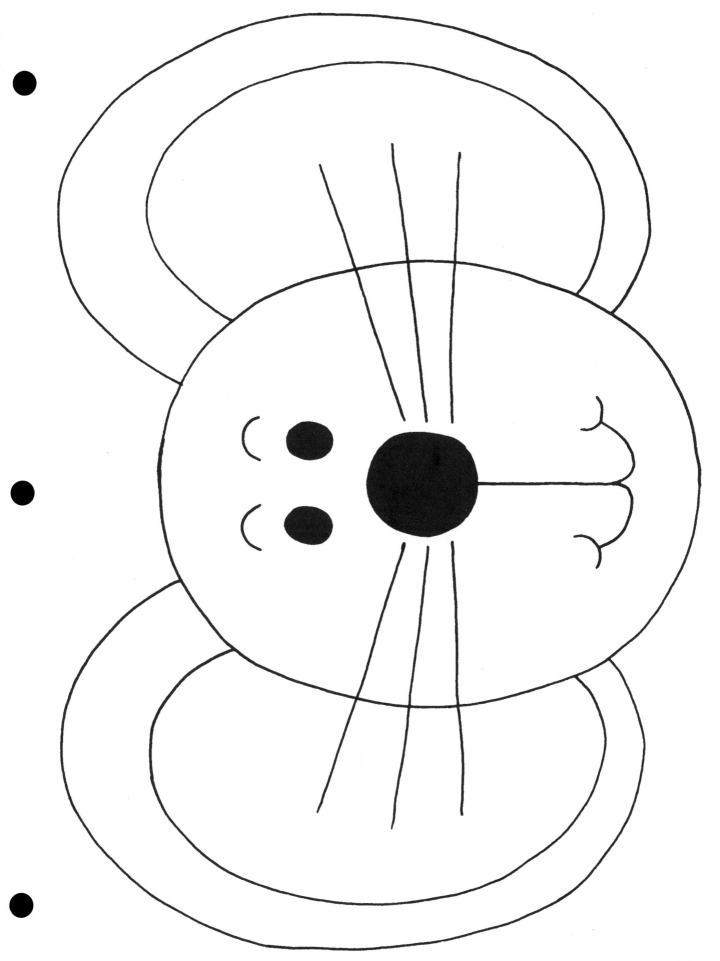

 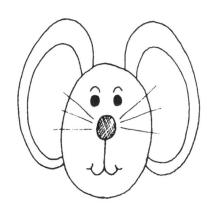

12

"Not I," said

_____ _____.

"Not I," _____

_____ _____.

“   ”

_____   _____→)   _____

_____   _____ .

"Then I will," said

the _____ _____ _____.

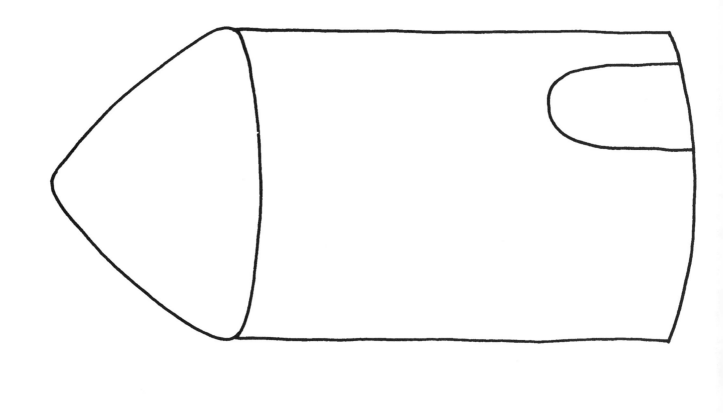

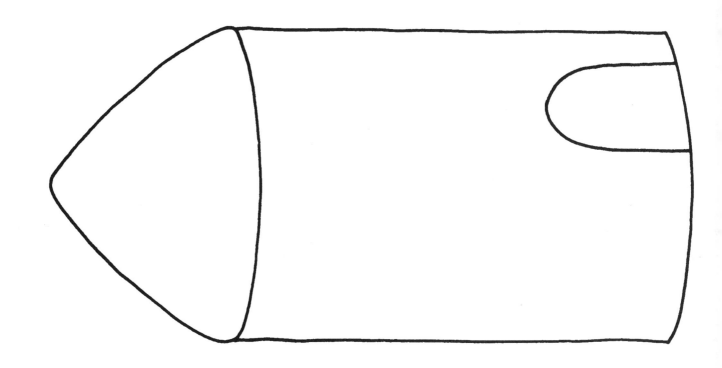

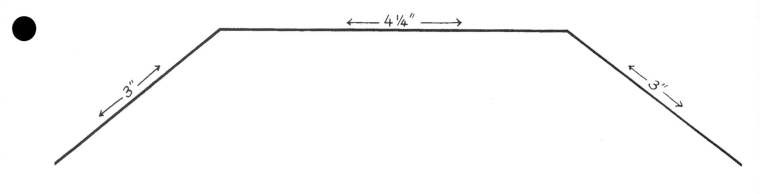

← 4 ¼" →

3"

3"

← 9" → (run to edge of construction paper)

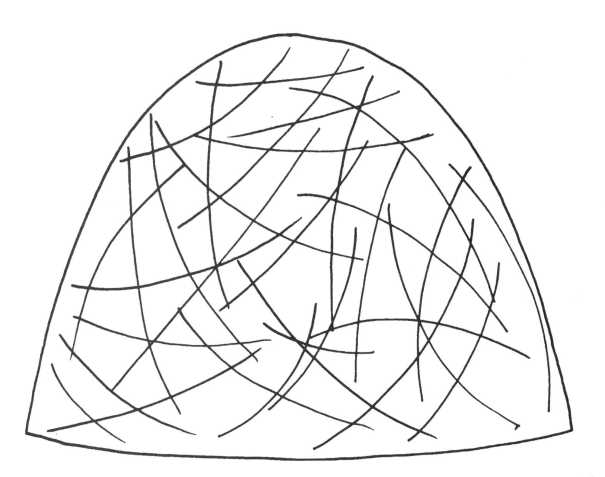

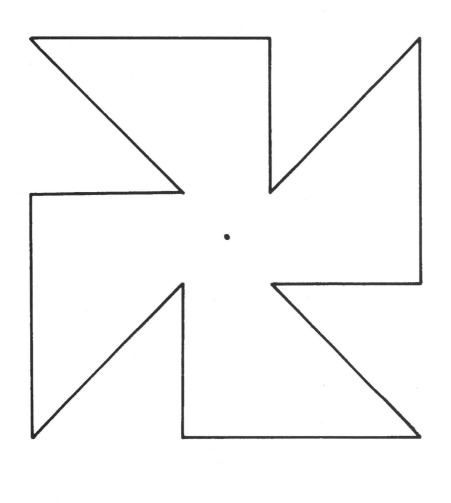

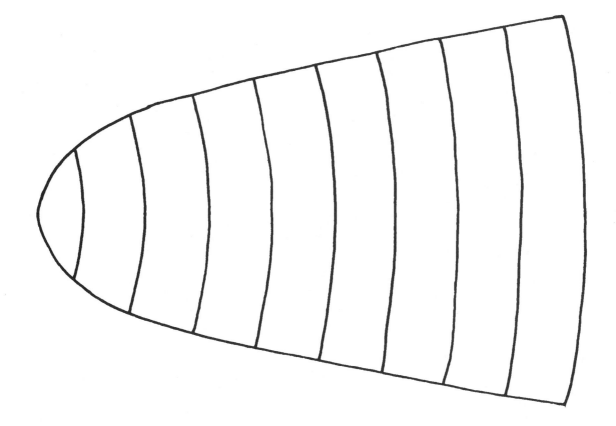

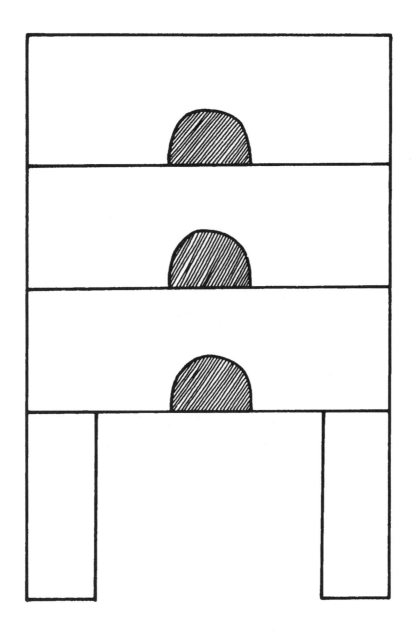

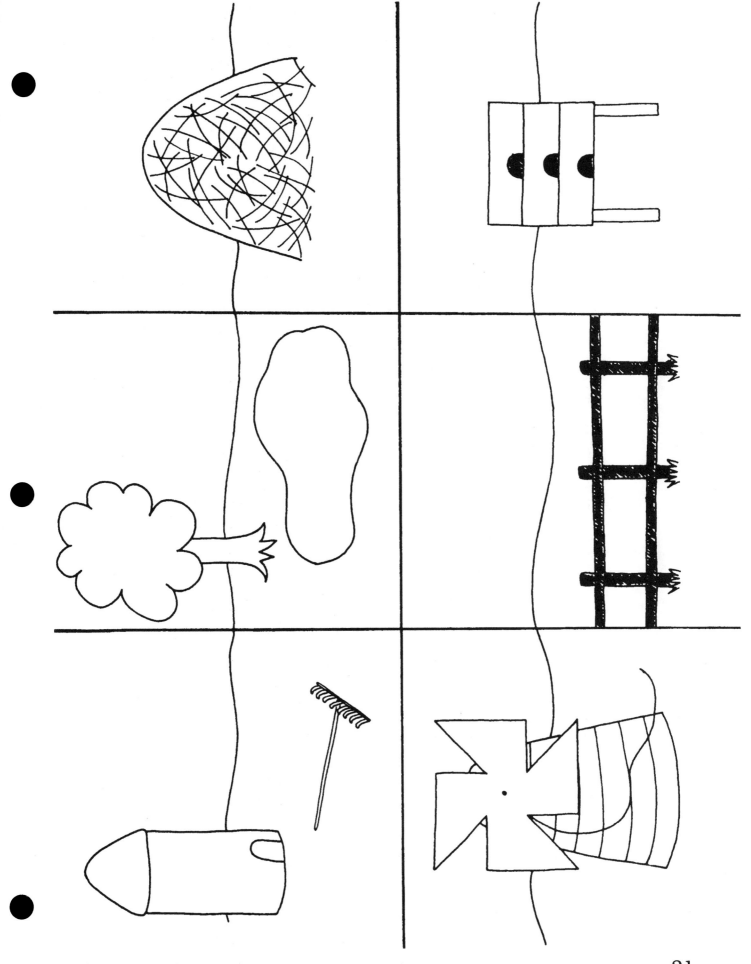

22

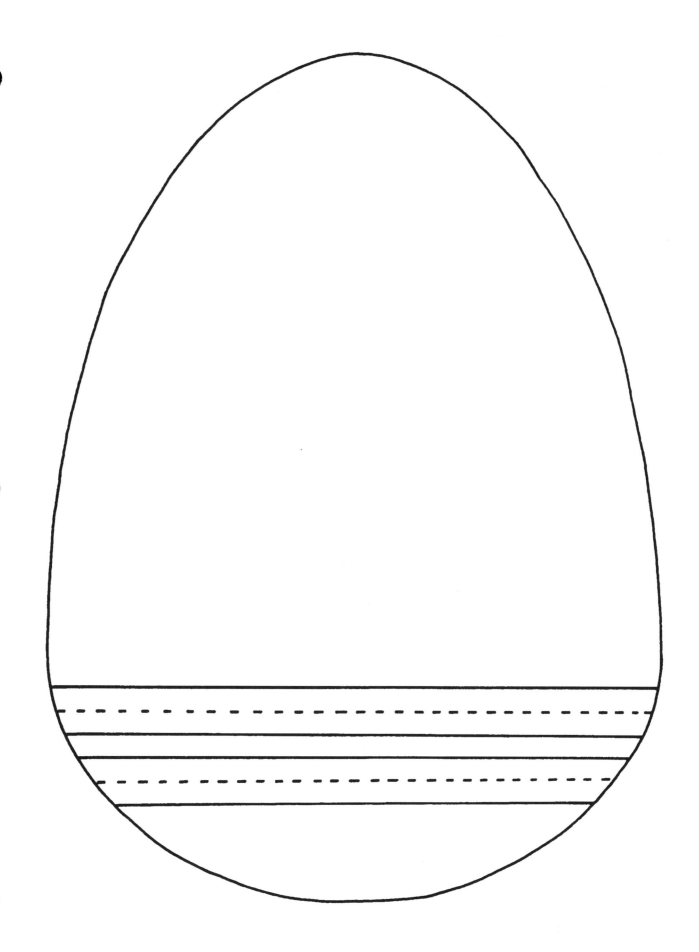

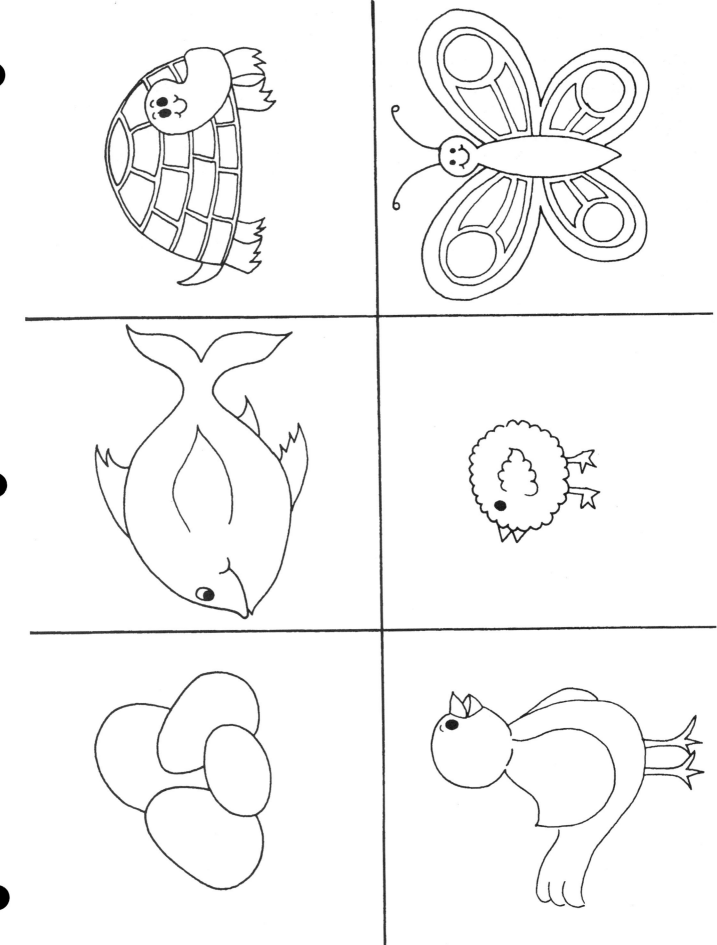

24

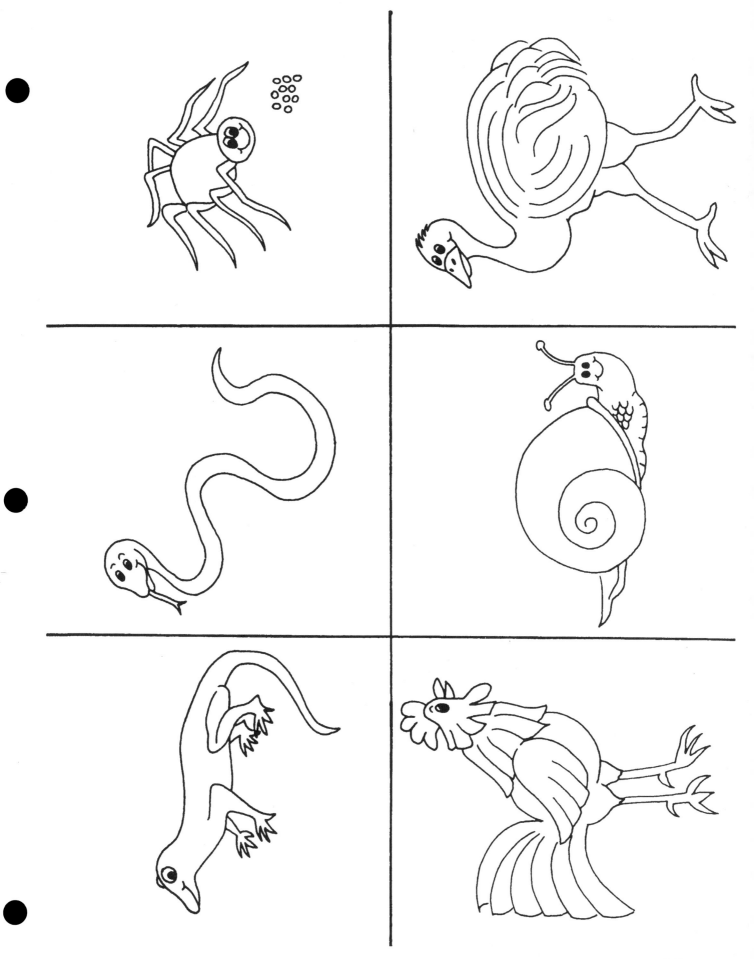

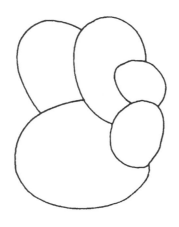

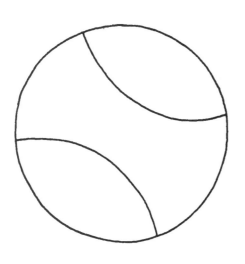

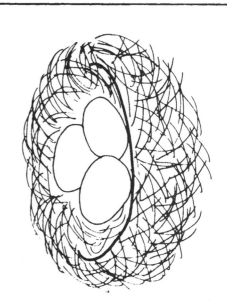

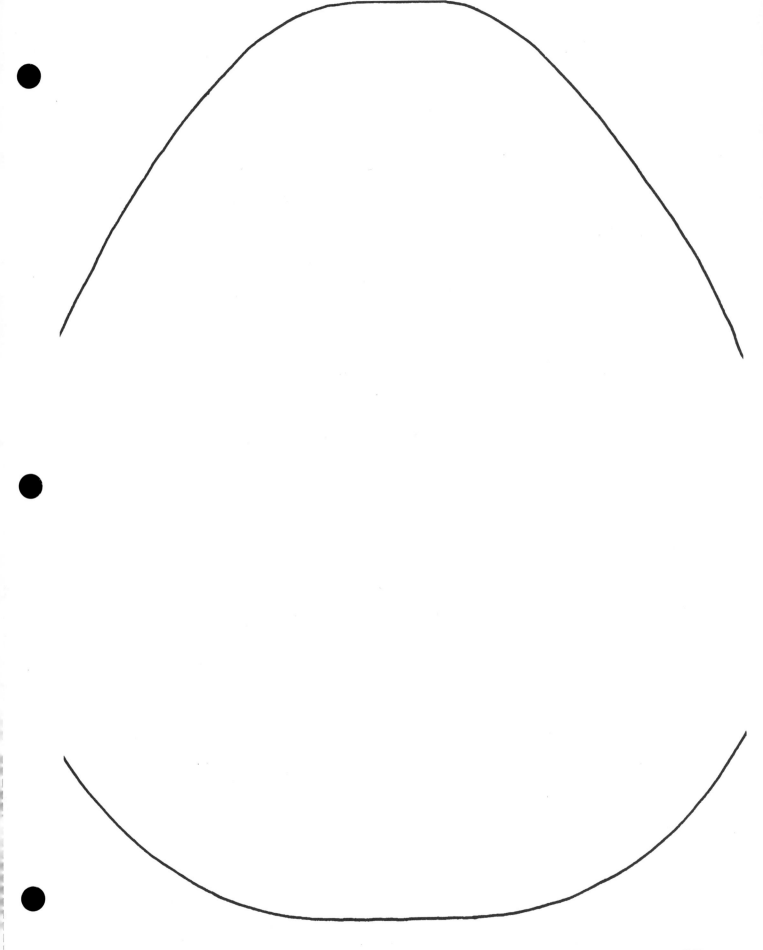

On Monday out came

X

Seven Eggs

by _____

On Wednesday
out came

x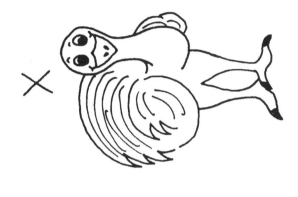

On Tuesday
out came

x

On Friday
out came

×

On Thursday
out came

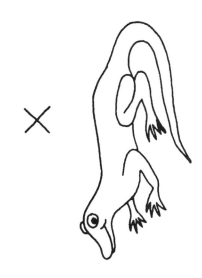

×

On Sunday
out came

×

On Saturday
out came

×

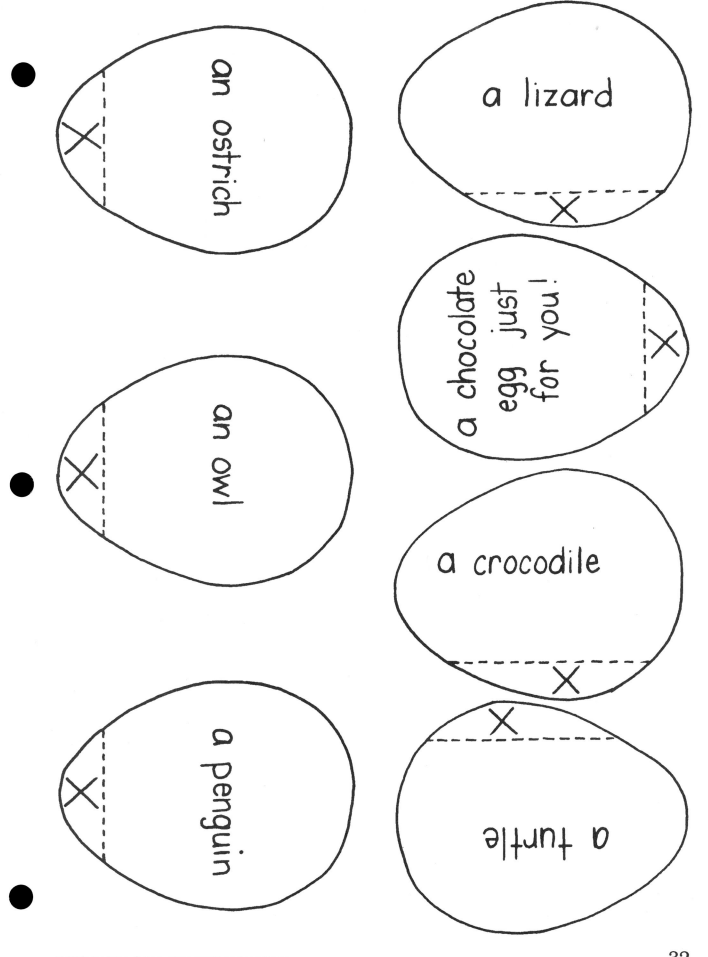

an ostrich

a lizard

an owl

a chocolate egg just for you!

a crocodile

a penguin

a turtle

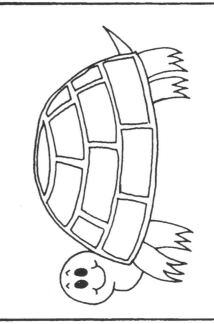

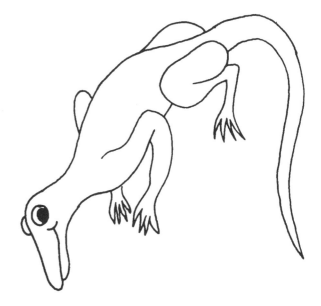

33

mother hen

cover pictures

The Chicken Book

37

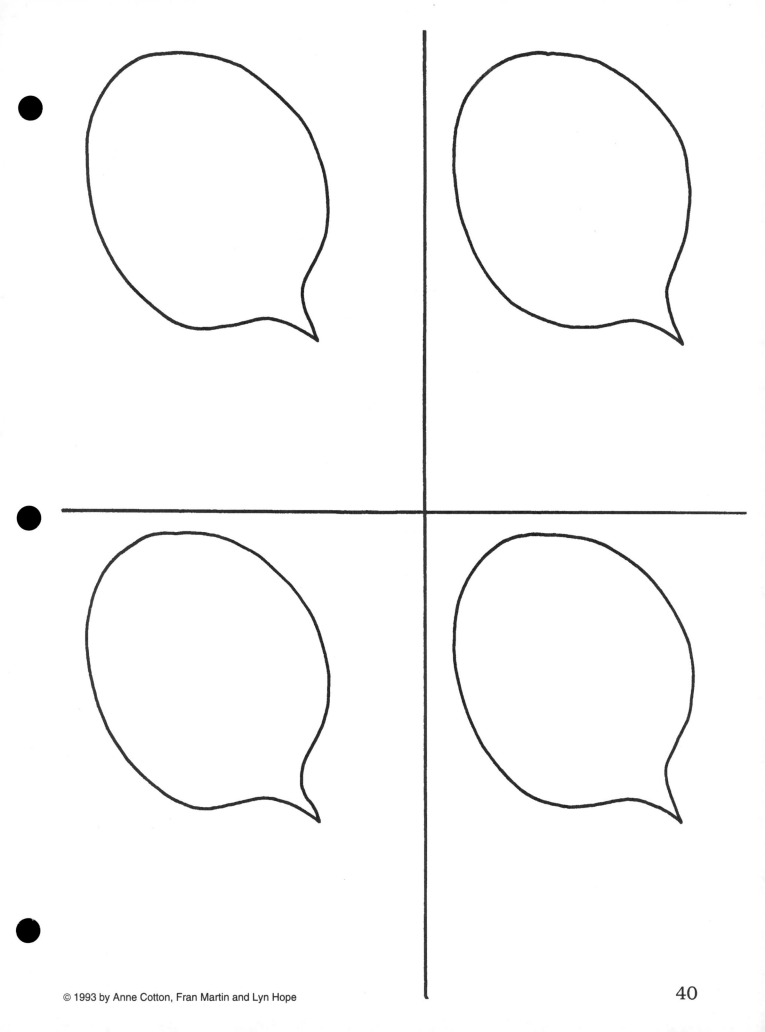

Humpty Dumpty sat on a wall

Humpty Dumpty had a great fall

All the king's horses

And all the king's men

Couldn't put Humpty together again.

Humpty Dumpty sat on a wall

Humpty Dumpty had a great fall

All the king's horses

And all the king's men

Couldn't put Humpty together again.

Humpty Dumpty

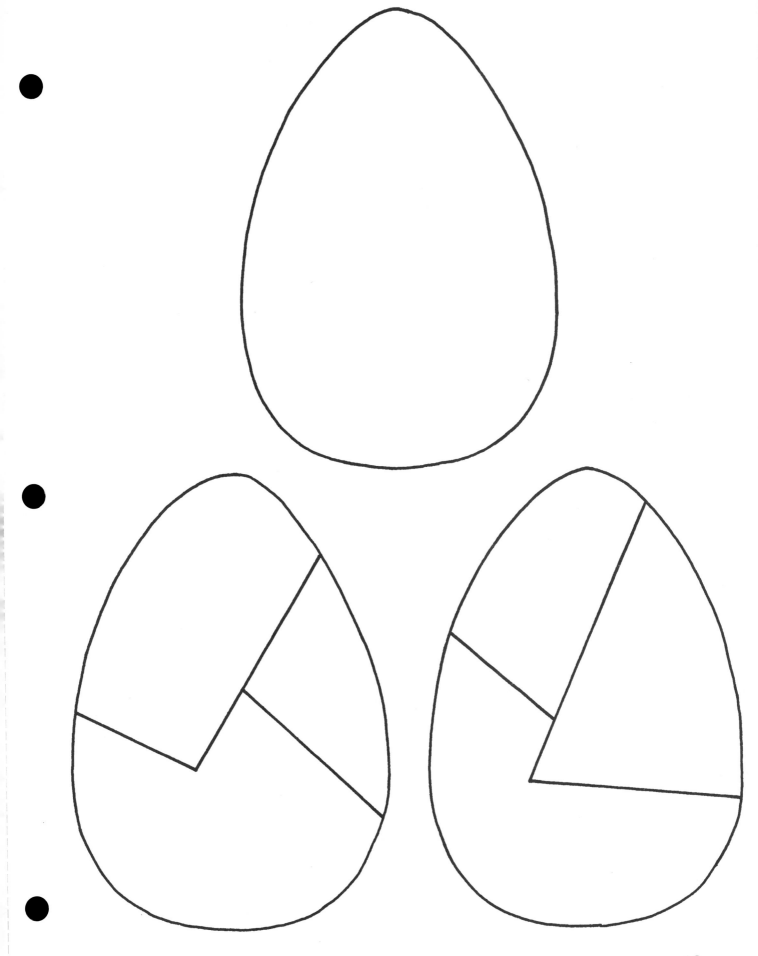

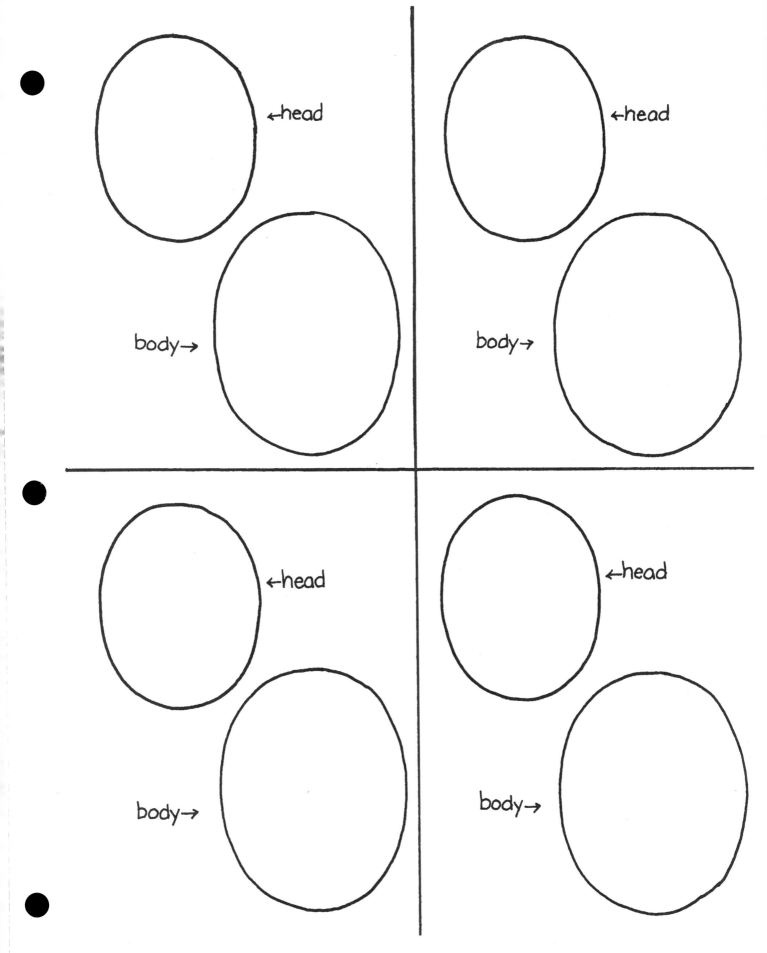

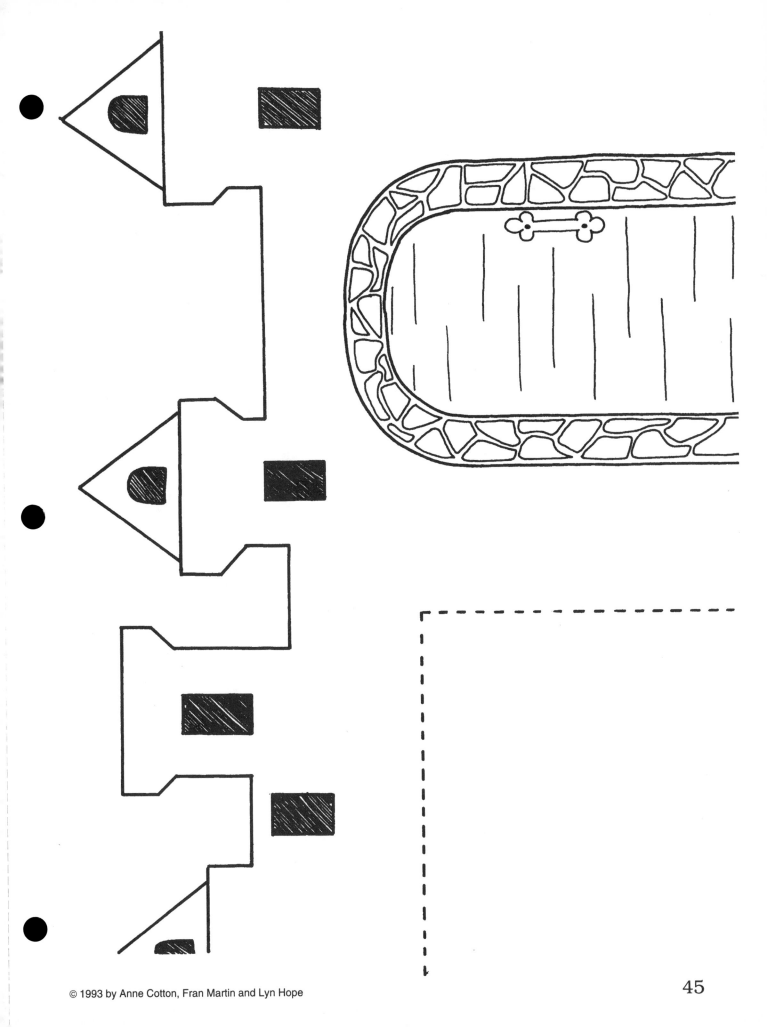

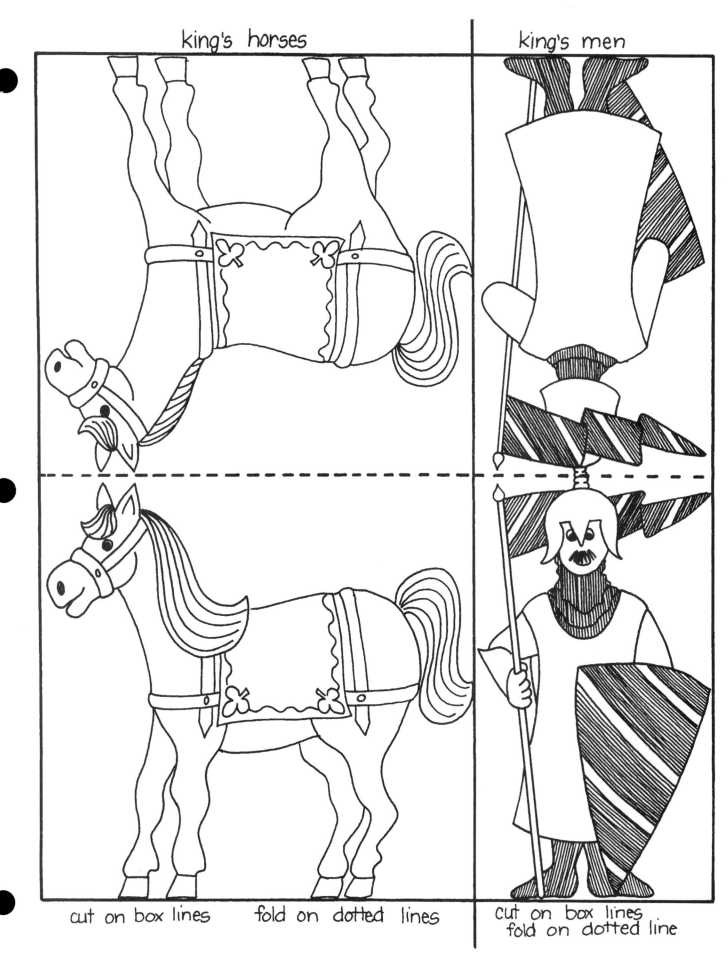

cut on box lines   fold on dotted lines

cut on box lines
fold on dotted line

back of wall   back of wall

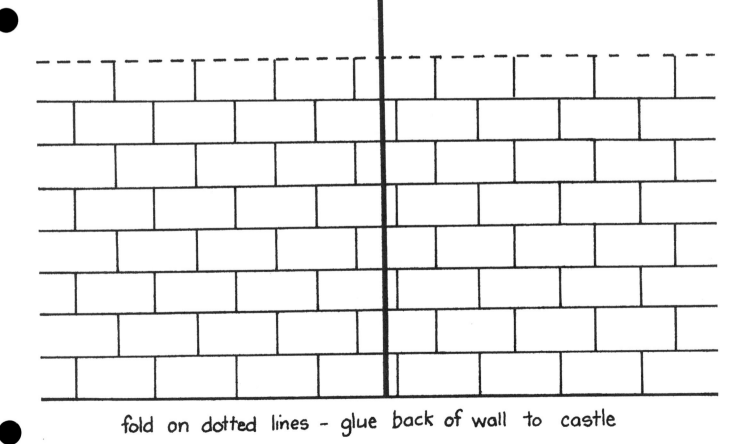

fold on dotted lines - glue back of wall to castle

soon little chickies

Mother Hen

bright sunshine

Eggs in a Nest

cover

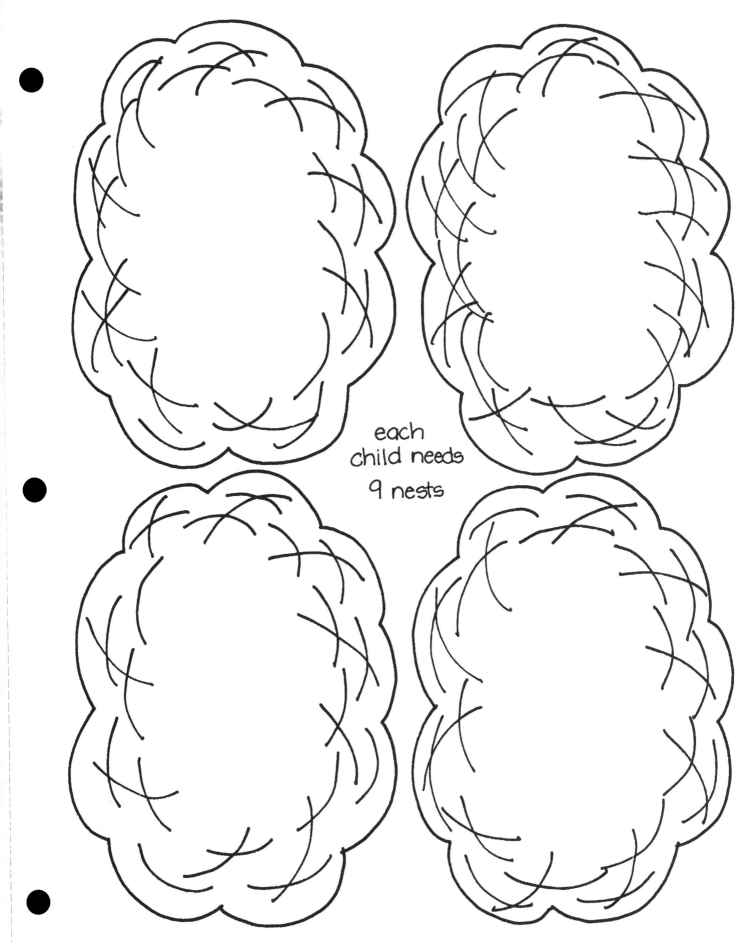

each
child needs
9 nests

53

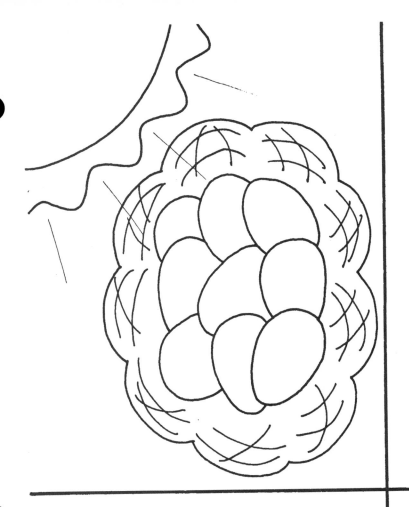

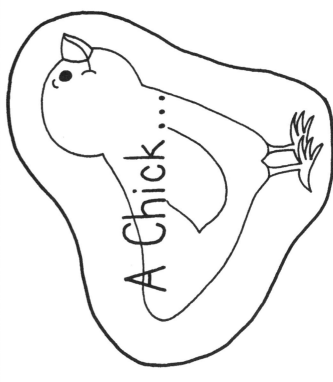

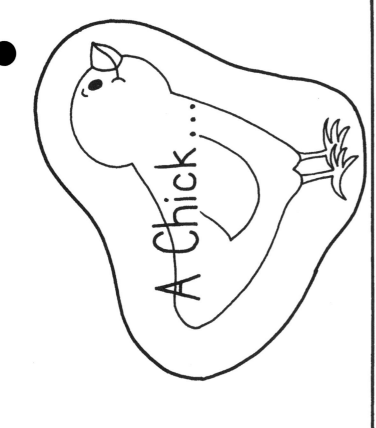

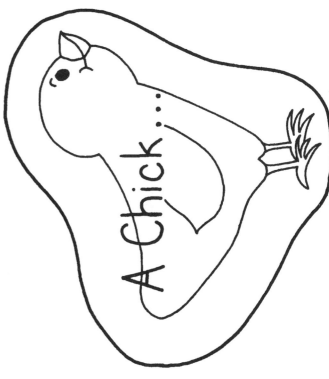

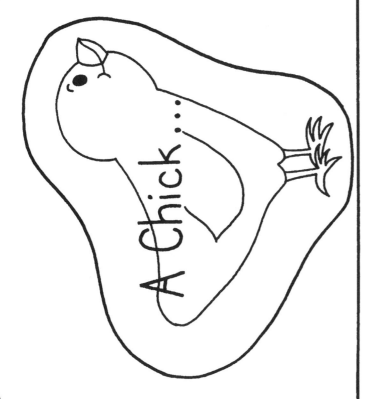

by _____

by _____

60

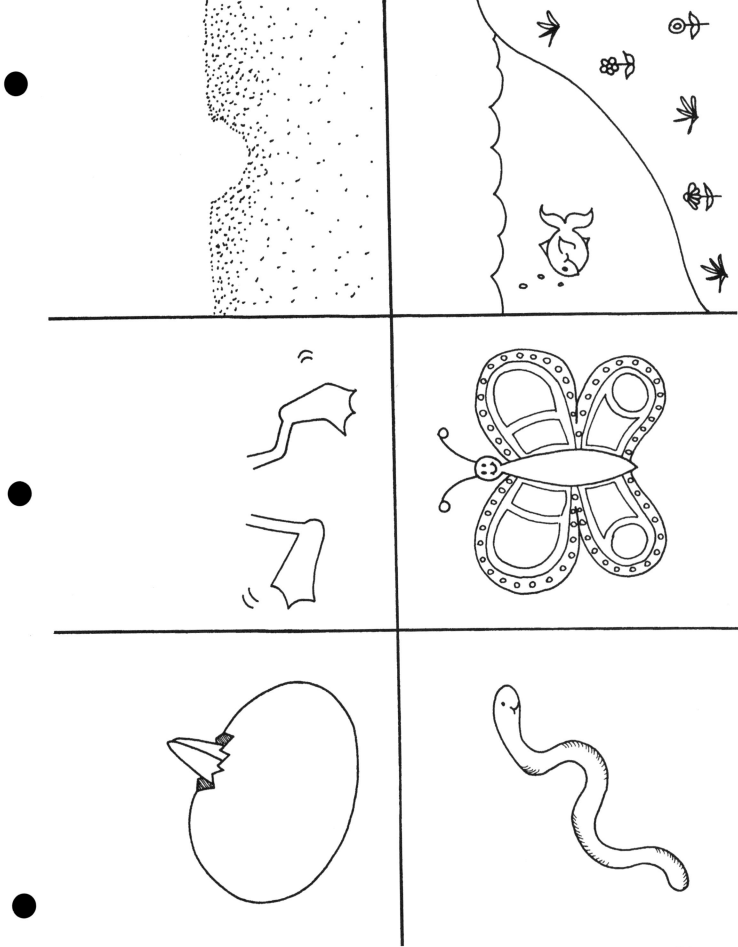

61

Where's the Egg?

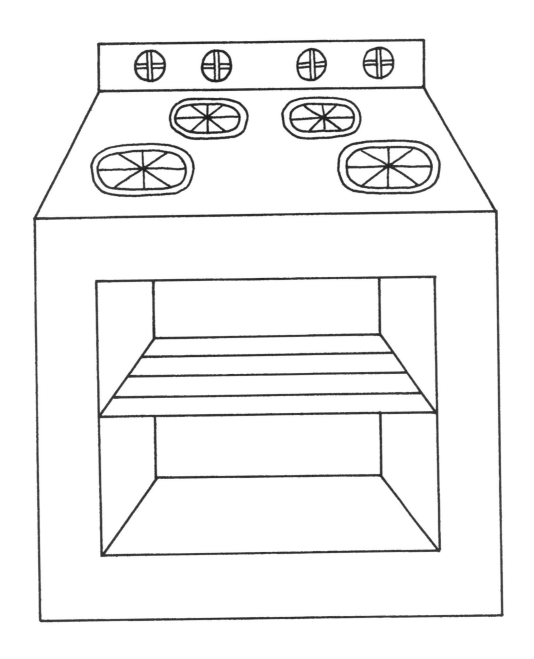

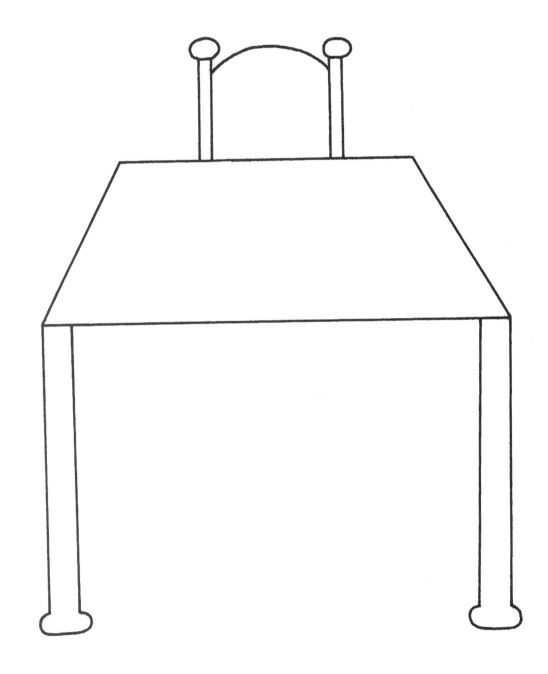

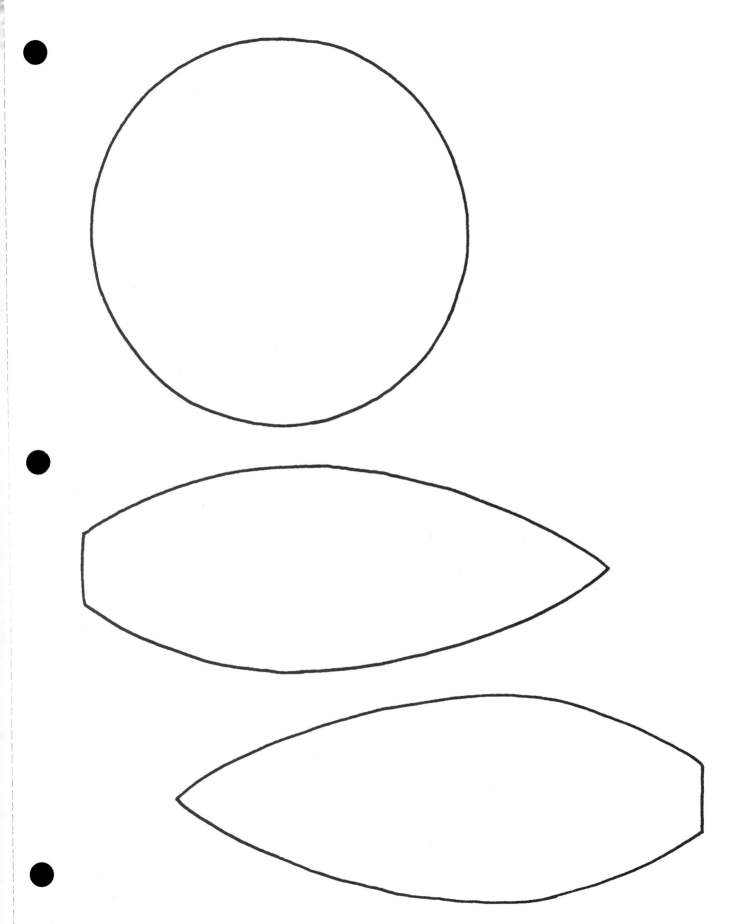

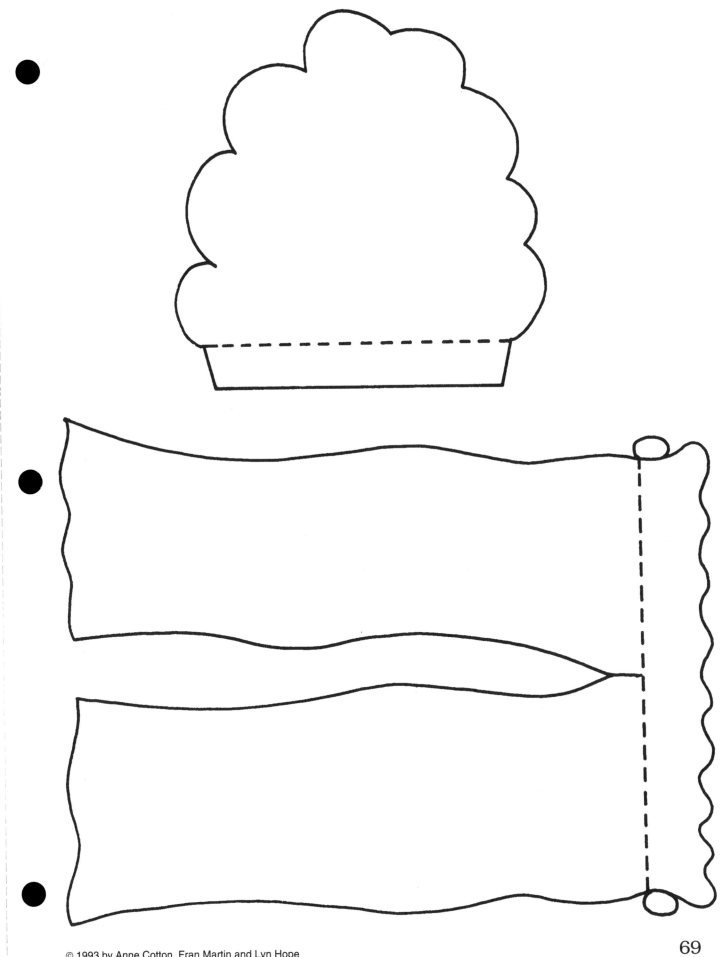

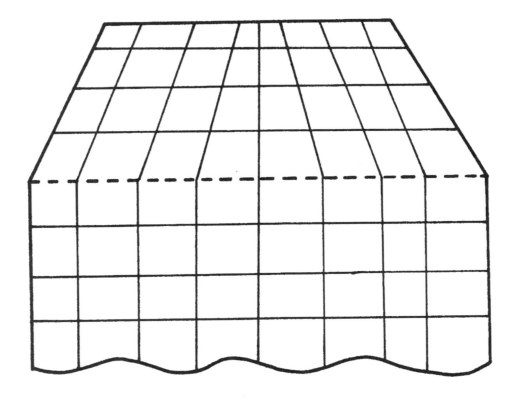

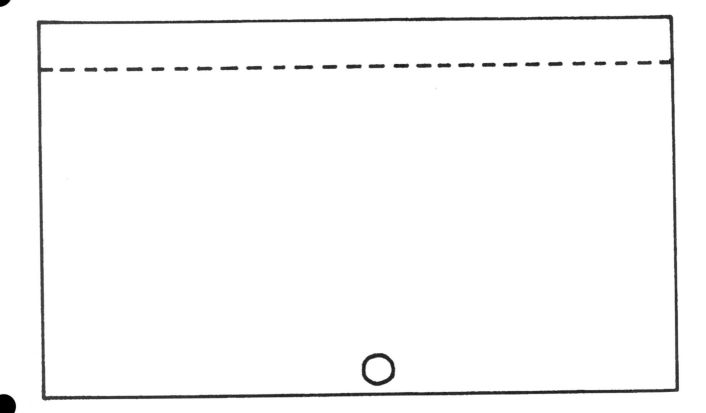

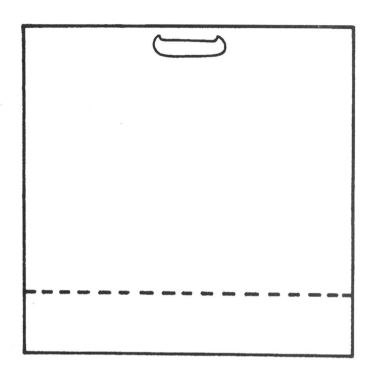

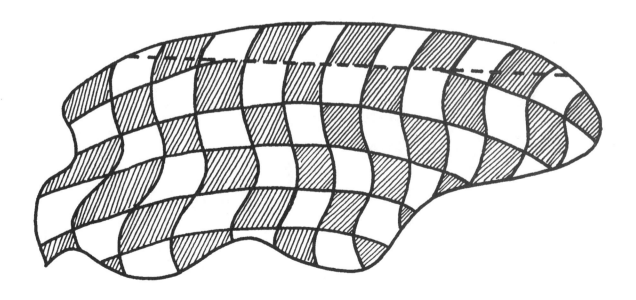

Bunny was sad.

He lost his egg.

He looked inside the oven.

He looked under the table.

He looked in the closet.

He looked behind the drapes.

He looked inside the basket.

He found his egg.

Bunny was happy.

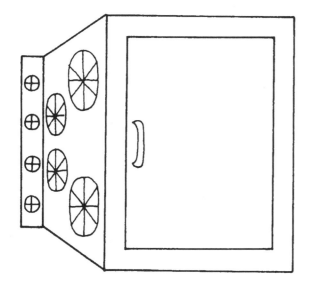

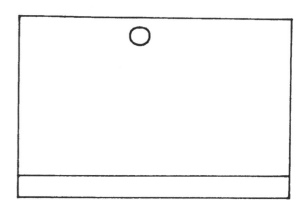

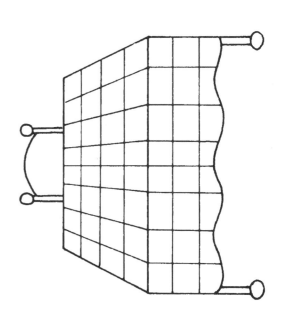

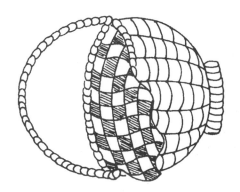

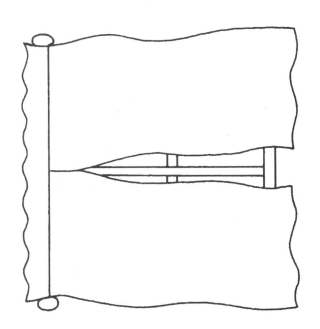

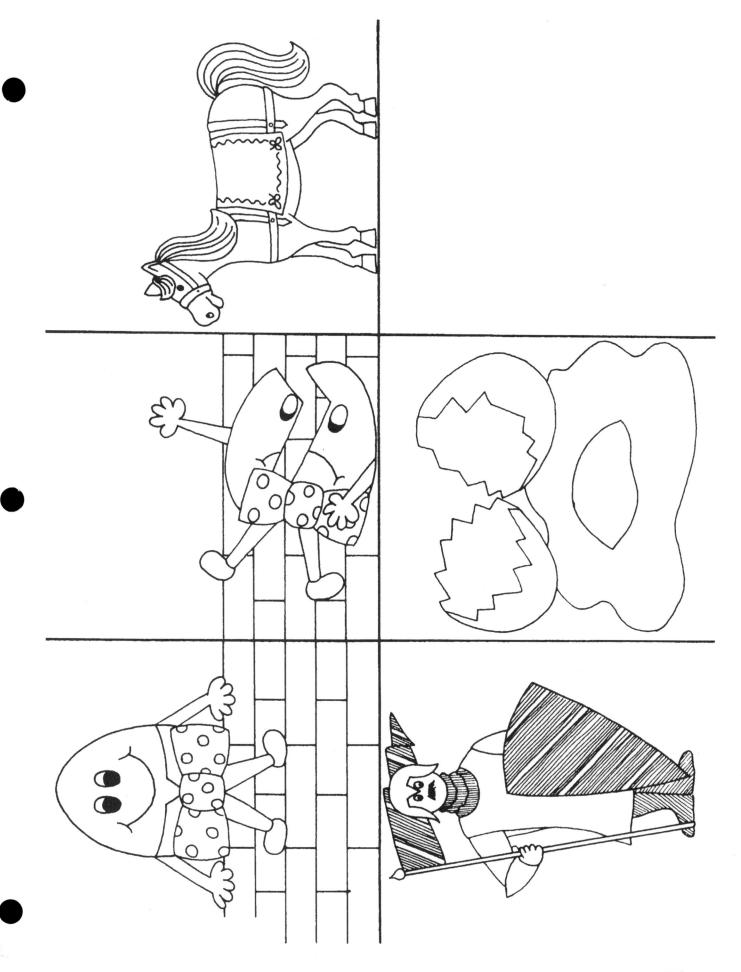